The Practice of Christian Perfection

Crucified Love

Robin Maas

Abingdon Press / Nashville

CRUCIFIED LOVE
The Practice of Christian Perfection

This book is printed on acid-free paper.

Library of Congress Cataloging-in-Publication Data

Maas, Robin, 1939–
   Crucified love : the practice of Christian perfection / Robin
Maas.
      p.   cm.
   Bibliography: p.
   ISBN 0-687-10009-7 (alk. paper)
   1. Perfection—Religious aspects—Christianity. 2. God—Love.
3. God—Worship and love. 4. Spiritual life. I. Title.
BT766.M24   1989
248.4'82—dc19   89-190
                                                            CIP

Scripture quotations, except paraphrases, or unless otherwise indicated, are from *The Jerusalem Bible*, Reader's Edition, copyright © 1966 by Darton, Longman & Todd, Ltd., and Doubleday, a division of Bantam, Doubleday, Dell Publishing Group, Inc. Reprinted by permission.

Scripture quotations noted RSV are from the Revised Standard Version of the Bible, copyright 1946, 1952, 1971 by the Division of Christian Education of the National Council of Churches of Christ in the U.S.A. Used by permission.

for Gabriel

MANUFACTURED BY THE PARTHENON PRESS AT
NASHVILLE, TENNESSEE, UNITED STATES OF AMERICA

— CONTENTS —

CONTENTS

The real problem of Christian Holiness, or sanctity, does not lie in the choice of an attitude toward the world; it lies in the recognition that Something has occurred, Someone has given himself up for us; this is what day by day changes us, our attitudes, our faces.

Luigi Giussani, Morality: Memory and Desire

Have you faith in Christ?"

"Are you going on to perfection?"

"Do you expect to be made perfect in love in this life?"

"Are you earnestly striving after it?"

These are the first of the disciplinary questions put to ordinands seeking full connection with The United Methodist Church. They are John Wesley's questions, and they indicate the importance he gave to the concept of Christian perfection, the growth in grace which comes through faithful Christian discipleship. As a doctrine, it was his most distinctive theological contribution to the church. As a way of life, it was the mark of his spiritual leadership. Unfortunately, it is also the part of his legacy that has been least understood; so much so, that later generations of Methodists have found the doctrine difficult to comprehend and even more difficult to follow. On occasions such as ordination services, it is given respect or even deference. Seldom, however, is it affirmed.

This was not always so. There was a time when every Methodist, clergy and lay alike, not only would have understood these disciplinary questions, but also would have had ready answers. Because there once was a time when Methodists held themselves mutually accountable for their progress in the Christian life. They did this at their weekly class meetings, where they told one another about their spiritual walk with Christ, and helped one another live out their discipleship. In Wesley's own words, they "watched over one another in love," and thereby grew in the knowledge and love of God—the path to perfection.

The guidelines for this spiritual journey were the General Rules of 1743, which prescribed a twofold method for faithful Christian discipleship: "works of mercy" and "works of piety." On the one hand, Methodists were to do all they could to serve God and their neighbor, while avoiding those things they knew were an offense to God and their neighbor. On the other hand, they were to practice the time-honored spiritual disciplines of the church: public worship, the Lord's Supper, the ministry of the word, private prayer, searching the scriptures, and fasting or abstinence. They adopted this twofold method with integrity, and thus their nickname became their identity. They became known as Methodists because they were methodical.

Their method, however, had purpose and direction. These early Methodists knew where they were headed, and it was not toward personal impeccability nor yet toward social utopia. They aspired first and foremost to the perfect love of an unbroken relationship with God. They were well aware that this would result in a radical transformation of their lives, both personal and social. But they did not put the cart before the horse. The priority was their covenant relationship with God. And they understood, as do all experienced Christian disciples, that this relationship has to be nurtured. It does not develop as a matter of course.

Accordingly, they sought the closest possible union with

Jesus Christ, the author and perfector of their covenant faith. They bound themselves to an obedient, methodical discipleship, and they took the simple precaution of holding one another accountable, not for spiritual accomplishments, but for a goal at once more modest and demanding: sustaining their communion with God. This was the perfection they sought, and they monitored their progress toward it with care; for their path was fraught with the resistance of human sin in all its forms.

That the doctrine has lost its status as a tradition is a sobering spiritual symptom. There are branches of the Methodist family where it is still given disciplinary, if not pastoral, prominence. But in The United Methodist Church, the mother church of Methodism, it is little taught and even less practiced. This is not for lack of information. There are a number of excellent studies available, including some fine contributions by younger Methodist scholars. For the most part, however, these approach the doctrine from a theological or historical perspective, making it relatively inaccessible to the rank and file of the church. And regrettably, many of the practical interpretations seem to be more concerned with the immediate needs of an emotionally enervated culture than with plain spiritual truth for plain people.

All of which makes this work by Professor Robin Maas shine like a pearl. Rarely can it be said that a book is both wise and beautiful. Yet these are the words which come to mind at every turn of the page. She gives new life to the doctrine of Christian perfection. In a context of enculturated Christianity, flanked on the one side by ecclesial self-maintenance and on the other by folk religiosity, she shows what it means to appropriate the fullness of our Christian heritage and at the same time be open to God's latest lavishment of grace. She gives us a perspective on holy living as the church has understood it throughout the ages, and then makes it relevant for today.

Moreover, although this is a book about John Wesley, by no means is he given center stage. Center stage belongs unequivocally to the Holy Spirit. As a result, we are given a compass that points us toward faithful discipleship in our own time, just as Wesley plotted a trustworthy course more than two centuries ago. Such historiographical clarity is rare in works of spiritual direction, and most welcome.

No less helpful and welcome is the clarity with which Dr. Maas defines Christian perfection. It is not the technique of personal fulfillment, for the first thing we discover in the spiritual life is that we are sinners, in need of forgiveness and reconciliation. Nor is it the self-love that domesticates God into personal experience, thereby reinforcing the chronic individualism of our culture. Nor yet is it superior spiritual knowledge, vaunted by those with the temerity to claim privileged access to God. It is none of these. Gently, but firmly, we are shown that Christian perfection is communion with God for God's own sake: an intimacy with God that enables us to love to our full capacity, because God loves us first. And the overwhelming reality of this love is that it pleads with us from the cross.

The wisdom of the book is that it disdains any shortcuts in the spiritual life, and clearly marks the pitfalls. Most especially does it expose the gnostic misunderstanding that communion with God is an effortless condition, effortlessly attained. Not that we must *earn* this relationship; God's grace is always a gift. But it is our responsibility to accept it, and most assuredly we must work to keep it. For sinful resistance is a subtle and persistent obstacle, requiring Christians to be constantly trusting and watchful. We must be open to grace with the simplicity of little children. We must fight resistance to grace with the craft of seasoned warriors.

Rightly discerning the common sense of the early Methodists in this regard, Dr. Maas shows how methodical obedience to Christ is the only way to sustain such a communion with God. There must be an intentional quest for spiritual perfection—a "Christification" of our lives—and a concomitant self-denial. She takes us step by step through what this demands of us in practical Christian living: the discipline of prayer (our "self-stripping" before God); the love of neighbor (the embodiment of our own salvation); personal accountability for sin (acknowledging the violation of our relationship with God); crucifixion of self (the practice of prudent asceticism); and the communion of saints (the supportive company of those on the journey with us). At each step there is a well-selected word from the spiritual classics of the church. But just as important are the author's own insights, calling us again and again to the perfection of loving God for God's own sake.

The beauty of the book lies in its quality of pristine spiritual writing. Those already on the path to perfection will recognize in Robin Maas a true spiritual companion. Those who are about to embark on the journey will sense in her a spiritual mentor. There is more here than a treatise on Christian perfection, and more than a devotional guide. What we have is a spiritual testimony, written with the authority of one who treads the path to perfection herself. As her witness unfolds, we learn firsthand what it is to know God, to commune with God, to "keep one's appointments with God" in prayer, and to "find our neighbor in God" as we serve. Such God-centeredness cannot be described. It can only be shared.

Crucified Love is nothing less than "A Plain Account of Christian Perfection" for today. Like Wesley's treatise of 1766, it is simple, straightforward, and steeped in the Scriptures and the Christian heritage. In brief, Robin Maas has reawakened tradition in the doctrine of perfect love for a new generation of Christian disciples. Methodists can own it again, if they will, and make it once more their spiritual gift to the church. Christians of all persuasions can practice it as they prepare for the coming Reign of God, on earth as in heaven.

David Lowes Watson
General Board of Discipleship
The United Methodist Church

— INTRODUCTION —

The chapters in this little book—with the exception of chapter 3, which was added later—were originally written and delivered as addresses to United Methodist clergy, specifically, to members of the Southern New England Conference who, in February 1988, gathered at the Mont Marie Retreat Center in Mount Holyoke, Massachusetts, for their annual Spiritual Formation Retreat. At the time I was invited to lead the retreat I was told that the previous year's retreat, led by David Lowes Watson of the General Board of Discipleship of The United Methodist Church, had focused on the concept and practice of "Covenant Discipleship." Covenant Discipleship is a program of spiritual renewal currently being sponsored by the denomination under the leadership of Dr. Watson and is based on John Wesley's original Methodist class meeting structure.

In the short time that Covenant Discipleship has been widely promoted and implemented in parishes and seminaries, it has generated remarkable interest in and enthusiasm for a more intentional and accountable practice of particular spiritual disciplines, especially those dear to the heart of John Wesley and the early Methodists: daily prayer, Bible study, frequent communion, fasting, works of mercy, and justice. My own involvement in initiating a program of Covenant Discipleship at Wesley Theological Seminary in Washington, D.C., has convinced me that this communal effort to recover a traditional spiritual practice is timely and effective—functioning, as it has, as part of a larger effort to reclaim a distinctive spirituality for a very large portion of Protestant Christians in America.

Under the circumstances, I felt it would make sense to design a retreat experience that would help clergy deepen their understanding and appreciation of the ecumenical significance of this particular spiritual practice by focusing on the historical and theological roots of the ancient spirituality that gave rise to it. United Methodists and other Wesleyan Christians may or may not know much about the doctrine of "Christian perfection"; but even those who do recognize it as a distinctively Wesleyan emphasis are often not aware of how important this doctrine has been throughout the long history of the Church Universal. "Perfection," when it first captured the religious imagination of the young Oxford don John Wesley, already had a long and time-honored pedigree among those branches of Christianity that treasure a vision of salvation that is consummated in *holiness*—that would not merely have us forgiven of our sins but rid of them as well. It was Wesley's special gift and genius to interpret this "Catholic" doctrine for Protestant spiritual practice, first, by coherently integrating it with the doctrine of justification by faith and, second, by popularizing a concrete ecclesial structure—the class meeting—as a way to provide communal support for each individual who had chosen, in obedience to Christ, to "go on to perfection."

It is, I am convinced, vitally important that we

American Christians acquire a longer and more
discriminating memory. It is frankly risky to adopt a
spirituality or a given spiritual practice simply because it
is novel, or even because it seems to "work." Our prayer
life should reflect what we believe to be *true*—and not
simply consoling—about the nature of God, of Jesus
Christ, and of humankind. These reflections by a Roman
Catholic who happens to teach in a United Methodist
seminary are offered as one small contribution to the
effort to lengthen that collective memory and to help
persuade Wesleyan colleagues, students, and friends
that the straight and narrow path to perfection we tread
together is ultimately an "inclusive" one.

My gratitude to Bishop George Bashore and his staff,
especially to the Reverend Richard Wiborg, with whom
I worked closely in preparing for the retreat, and to the
members of the Southern New England Conference,
who listened patiently to, struggled with, and digested
at least some of all this abounds.

Robin Maas
Wesley Theological Seminary
Washington, D.C.

1

Christian Perfection in Christian Tradition

If you wish to be perfect, go and sell what you own and give the money to the poor, and you will have treasure in heaven; then come, follow me. (Matt. 19:21)

There is a very familiar advertising jingle that begins, "Be all that you can be" and ends, "in the Army." The tune is catchy and the message is utterly up-to-date. It is an accurate reflection of what most modern Americans believe is their highest calling: the attainment of personal fulfillment. Be all that *you*—this unique, one of a kind individual—can possibly be. Find yourself. Be good to yourself. Love yourself. Actualize your potential. Achieve.

This message is undeniably attractive, culturally pervasive, and therefore extremely powerful. Who would not want to be the best she could possibly be? Who would not want the best for himself and his family? We see personal excellence and self-actualization promoted and sought in every possible setting. The craze for dieting and physical fitness is a particularly obvious instance of this; so are workaholism, many forms of therapy, self-help and support groups, adult education classes, and the like. Both the electronic and printed media invite us at every turn to examine ourselves to discover what our "needs" are and then urge us aggressively to meet them. You can do it! You should do it! There is something wrong with you if you don't do it!

The demand for perfection in every aspect of our lives whips and drives us as though we were a team of horses; but for the most part, we do not rebel. Instead, we acquiesce in the expectation that we should and can make more of ourselves than we do. We look for the perfect job, the perfect mate, and we wonder what is wrong with us when we cannot find the satisfaction we seek in work or family life. We want to be perfect and we want our children to be perfect. Science has discovered a technique for detecting imperfect children still in the womb, and more often than not, such children—once detected—are aborted. A less than perfect child will have a less than perfect life.

It is easy for clergy and other serious Christians to recognize this virtuous-sounding hedonism in the broader culture and deplore it. It doesn't take too much theological sophistication to recognize in this hot pursuit of personal perfection and fulfillment a neo-Pelagianism or works-righteousness that seeks to control and ensure "salvation"—whatever that may mean. What is not so easy is to see the way in which this very same preoccupation with self-improvement insinuates itself into the church, into the preaching, teaching, and counseling of the clergy, and into the personal spiritual practice and public witness of the laity.

For example: We have seen *ad nauseam* descriptions of the "effective pastor." The church expects its religious professionals to be good preachers, teachers, counselors, community organizers, and fundraisers—as if somehow these excellent activities taken together add up to that very elusive but desirable good: ministry. It is hard to recognize the ways in which secular cultural values mask themselves in religious jargon, for in this masking we seek and give ourselves permission to "be all that we can be." Certainly we all very much want to "be"—and the more we can be the better.

Or consider the restless and persistent quest of the laity for a church that will somehow fulfill all their social and spiritual needs. The phenomenon of "church shopping" in which entertaining preaching and lively education and social programs are inspected like so much merchandise has become increasingly common, almost a taken-for-granted procedure, resorted to whenever a family moves or an individual becomes offended as a consequence of a real or imagined slight.

As a seminary professor very much concerned with issues of religious identity and spiritual formation, I am conscious of the ways in which theological education has also been seduced by the cultural values of personal excellence and self-fulfillment. I see it most, perhaps, in an attitude toward preparation for ministry that focuses very much on individual attainment of technical expertise and promotes this by the use of theological language. The very common request that seminarians and candidates for ministry—Protestant and Catholic both—attend to discovering their own "gifts and graces" is a case in point. Let me try to explain.

Talk about gifts and graces reflects an approach to spiritual and ministerial formation that entails a process I have heard described as "exfoliation."[1] It is a bit like peeling away the layers of an onion in an attempt to get to an inner core. Likewise, there are theories of pedagogy and human development that posit an inner core—a unique individual being—whom, if we are patient and persistent enough, we can uncover or discover. It or he or she already exists and merely needs to be known. But those of us who peel and chop onions have learned that there is no "core" to speak of, just layer after layer, and working our way through the layers is usually an occasion for tears.

Of course it is true that there is much about ourselves we do not yet know but need to know; some of us have discovered hidden talents. Fewer of us have discovered hidden character flaws, yet these unpleasant discoveries are every bit as important in preparing us for faithful discipleship and ministry—perhaps more so. What I would like to suggest is that spiritual formation in the truest and oldest sense of the word is rather different from this more modern quest for personal integrity or authenticity. It *is* a quest for "wholeness" (another popular modern term), but the traditional Christian standard for wholeness is not self-fulfillment.

What is it then? Christians who worship and minister out of a Wesleyan history and grounding are in theory, and should be in practice, closely allied with the traditional Christian vision of wholeness, which goes by the name "Christian perfection." It is still the case that United Methodist ministers, for example, solemnly declare at their ordination that they are "going on to perfection." What Christians in this tradition may not remember, or may not fully realize, is that this ideal of the spiritual life did not originate with John Wesley. It is a very old, very biblical, very monastic vision of spiritual life and, until the twentieth century, has been the dominant vision of what spiritual maturation means—at least in the Wesleyan, Anglican, Eastern Orthodox, and Roman Catholic traditions.

Whereas the modern personality seeks fulfillment through an "uncovering" or process of self-discovery, the early Christians sought fulfillment—or rather, *completion*—through a process of formation, that is, through a kind of shaping or molding of the self. The self was recognized as an insistent, aggressive, demanding reality that was already there. It did not need to be discovered. It needed to be recast or, in the language of scripture, reborn. Made anew.

Now, any molding or shaping presupposes a model— something to which the object being shaped must conform. And for the early church there was no question about what this was to be: The model governing the shaping was Jesus Christ. More particularly, it was Jesus Christ crucified: divine Love, sacrificing itself for the other—for the unredeemed. Individual uniqueness had nothing to do with it. And neither did talent. What needed to be uncovered was sin.

Despite the widespread cultural craze for a perfect body, a perfect mate, a perfect job, and perfect children, modern Christians are very uncomfortable with the word *perfection*. In fact, if there is one area of life in which contemporary Christians are likely to eschew perfection, it is in religion. Here we are quick to label ourselves "sinners." Here, more than in any other area of life, we are ready to expect less of ourselves rather than more.

The same was true of many of John Wesley's Protestant contemporaries—especially those strongly influenced by the continental Reformers, Luther and Calvin. Over and over he was urged by colleagues and critics to abandon the term "Christian perfection" for something more palatable, yet he stubbornly—some would say perversely—insisted on retaining it. Difficult though the term may be, I am glad that he did. Because in doing so, Wesley was insisting on fidelity to this longer tradition, which says that spiritual maturation, spiritual growth, is not a purely subjective process between God and the individual that can never be judged by external or communal standards. In clinging to the ideal of Christian perfection, Wesley was claiming, first, a biblical, christological norm for spiritual growth, second, a traditional, communal norm, and third, an objective, changeless—and therefore countercultural—norm.

Perfection as a Biblical-Christological Norm

Let us begin with what scripture has to say about perfection. In the Hebrew scriptures, the word commonly translated with the English word *perfect* is *tamim*. It means whole, sound, unblemished—as in the case of a sacrificial offering, which must be perfect. Perfection is also something ascribed to God, whose knowledge and work, especially the *Torah*, are perfect (Deut. 32:4; Ps. 19:7). But human beings could also be perfect. Job was perfect—or blameless—especially in his meticulous fulfillment of his cultic or religious observations; and so was Noah (Gen. 6:9). God expected Abraham to be perfect or blameless (Gen. 17:1). In fact the Bible is full of references to the possibility of perfection in humankind, but this has been largely lost to the modern reader since many of the newer translations replace the earlier word *perfect* (as it appears in the Old Testament of the King James Version) with words such as *blameless* or *righteous*. But however the word is translated, it is clear that this is what God expects from us, that this expectation is not an impossible one, and that perfection has much to do with obedience. As it is written in Deuteronomy:

> For this Law that I enjoin on you today is not beyond your strength or beyond your reach. It is not in heaven, so that you need to wonder, "Who will go up to heaven for us and bring it down to us, so that we may hear it and keep it?" Nor is it beyond the seas, so that you need to wonder, "Who will cross the seas for us and bring it back to us, so that we may hear it and keep it?" No, the Word is very near to you, it is in your mouth and in your heart for your observance.   (30:11-14)

And what the Lord Yahweh expects, Jesus Christ expects. But with Jesus, we see that perfection entails more than obedience. The rich young man who wishes to gain eternal life has certainly lived an exemplary life. He is a "good" person—perhaps a fine person. He too has been meticulously obedient to all the commandments. Yet Jesus tells him that this is not enough. "If you wish to be perfect," he says, "go and sell what you own and give the money to the poor, and you will have treasure in heaven; then come, follow me" (Matt. 19:21).

Obedience to the commandments, important as it is, costs this good young man nothing. But when he hears that the quest for perfection will cost him his possessions, he falters and withdraws. Along with obedience to God comes self-denial. Notice that Jesus is not saying the young man must give away his possessions for the sake of the poor. He must give them away for his *own* sake—for the sake of what scripture calls perfection or "wholeness"—for the sake of his soul. Renouncing those things with which we cushion our existence, with which we keep dependence and necessity at arm's

length, is, according to the New Testament, spiritually
healthy.

Since the average Christian, clergy or lay, is not a rich
person, we might be excused for thinking that this
passage does not pose a special problem for us, but let's
be honest: We all continue to flee vulnerability of almost
every kind in our lives. The invitation of Jesus to
perfection is an invitation to give up everything—and
anything—to follow him. If the young man had not been
wealthy but had, say, clung to some other human
comfort, then the command issued would have been a
command to renounce *that* last hedge against vulnerability. What this text tells us is that perfection is a form of
nakedness. Nothing is to stand between us and God.

The most familiar New Testament passage on
perfection is undoubtedly that which concludes the
Sermon on the Mount: "You must therefore be perfect
just as your heavenly Father is perfect" (Matt. 5:48).
This injunction comes right after Jesus' uncomfortable
teaching about loving the way God loves: loving the
enemy. The use of the Greek word *teleios* in the New
Testament is particularly important for the traditional
Christian understanding of perfection. It means full-
grown, or whole—completed. So when Jesus uses this
word to summarize the divine demand to love the
enemy, he is linking perfection not only to love, but also
to a particular kind of love that is associated with God.

Love of enemies is not something that comes naturally
to human beings. It is, in fact, a most *un*natural thing to
do. This kind of love is natural only to God, and we
completely misunderstand him if we think Jesus is
talking here about love in the sense of warm, human
affection. He is not talking about feelings at all, but
about an act of the will—about the free choice to love

those who are harmful, hostile, and out to destroy us. What is alarming in this text is not that God can love like this (though that is hard enough to swallow), but that, clearly, the Lord expects *us* to be able to love like this. And this is not a suggestion; this is a command.

In Jesus, we see that perfection, although it includes obedience, involves more than the faithful fulfillment of religious obligation. In Jesus, we see that perfection entails a total commitment, the surrender of every last love that stands between us and our Maker. Perfection is about being *like God;* and being like God means *loving like God,* for God is Love. This may sound like an inspiring, compelling goal, but the love of enemies is an unnatural, selfless, sacrificial love. It does not promise us personal satisfaction or fulfillment.

The response of the early church to the command to be perfect was to look to Jesus, God Incarnate, as the model. The teachings of the carpenter-rabbi himself led them in this direction. "The disciple," said Jesus, "is not above his master: but every one that is perfect [the RSV says "fully taught"] shall be as his master" (Luke 6:40 KJV). The finished product will resemble the master craftsman himself. Paul, who makes use of the concept of perfection freely, understands this precisely. Speaking of the divine purpose in assigning diverse gifts for the building up of the church, he reminds the faithful in Ephesus that their fulfillment does not lie in their uniqueness—in being great preachers, teachers, or evangelists, necessary though these roles may be—but in their union *in Christ:*

> And to some, his gift was that they should be apostles; to some, prophets; to some, evangelists; to some, pastors and teachers; so that the saints together make a unity in

the work of service, building up the body of Christ. In
this way we are all to come to unity in our faith and in our
knowledge of the Son of God, until we become the
perfect Man, fully mature with the fullness of Christ
himself.   (Eph. 4:11-13)

This union is the fruit of a profound maturing in which
individual demands and needs are subordinated in
service to the building up of the Body. For Paul, the
perfect Christian is one whose faith has "ripened," so to
speak, because it is so deeply and firmly rooted in the
gospel of Christ crucified and risen. Such Christians are
no longer "children . . . tossed one way and another
and carried along by every wind of doctrine" (v. 14).
They are not easily seduced by the novel or the
"trendy"—by that which suggests we are saved by
anything other than the divine image and likeness
enfleshed in Jesus of Nazareth and stamped, if ever so
faintly, on our own contingent being.

This last point is especially important. When Paul
speaks of Jesus Christ as a model or measure for the
saints, he is not saying, "Here is a good person who
lives a good life. Try to be and do the same." It is true
that we must study the life of Jesus with patient, loving
attention because it mirrors for us at every point how
the Love that is God responds to the needs, and to the
sin, of the world. But remember, Paul never knew
Jesus of Nazareth while he walked this earth, nor does
he have anything to say about the ministry of Christ.
When Paul talks about Christ as the standard against
which we must measure ourselves, he is talking about
more than goodness—more even than greatness. He
is talking about sacrificial selflessness, about *crucified Love:*

> Think of God's mercy . . . and worship him, I beg you,
> in a way that is worthy of thinking beings, by offering
> your living bodies as a holy sacrifice, truly pleasing to
> God. Do not model yourselves on the behavior of the
> world around you, but let your behavior change,
> modeled by your new mind. This is the only way to
> discover the will of God and know what is good, what it
> is that God wants, what is the perfect thing to do.
>
> (Rom. 12:1-2)

This is not asking the impossible, according to Paul. This is what God intends.

When Paul tells the Philippians that he has willingly suffered the loss of all things for the sake of winning Christ (3:8), he is giving us the sequel to the story of the rich young man, who could give much but not all. In losing all, Paul sees the chance to win all. But he knows that in order to win Christ, he must allow himself to be reformed. He must submit himself to a shaping that will forever alter the configuration of his life. The path to perfection is a sharing, says Paul, in the sufferings of Christ by which we are "conformed" to Christ's death. That is the shape our life is to take. Paul tells us that our completion, our maturity, our destiny resides in the cross.

Perfection as a Traditional-Communal Norm

Throughout the following centuries, the church continued to study what scripture has to say about the ideal of perfection and to put it into practice as faithfully as it could. Although historical and cultural particularities sometimes governed how this ideal was interpreted, there was, over a period of many centuries, a surprising continuity in the way this tradition was transmitted.

To be specific, the identification of Christian perfection with love—not faith—but love, has been a constant; and, as we shall see, it is precisely this constant that authenticates John Wesley's understanding of perfection and places it squarely in the line of traditional orthodoxy.

Although all of the scriptures I've dealt with are important for the church's understanding and practice of the ideal of Christian perfection, no scripture is more central or significant than that of Luke 10:27. In answer to the scribe's devious question, "What must I do to inherit eternal life?" Jesus responds by directing him to the words of Hebrew scripture, so that the inquirer answers his own question: "You must love the Lord your God with all your heart, with all your soul, with all your strength, and with all your mind, and your neighbor as yourself." Jesus replies, "You have answered right . . . do this and life is yours." When the scribe presses him further by asking him to define what he means by "neighbor," Jesus recounts the parable of the Good Samaritan, thereby linking the idea of neighbor with that of the enemy—in this case, the ethnically impure and the heretical.

Although this passage nowhere mentions the word *perfection*, it was commonly understood by the church as *the* authoritative text for understanding the Christian ideal because it summarizes the divine demands and links them directly with the attainment of eternal life. In this text we have in capsule form the divine invitation to total self-giving addressed to the rich young man, as well as the command to love the unlovable—the enemy. In this passage the church heard the following message: If you would enter into eternal life, then you must love in the same way God loves—unreservedly, without limit. And it follows that if you as a human, a contingent being, would love as God loves, you must look to the Incarnation, to the crucified and risen Christ, as your model. No lesser love will do.

At the same time, the church assumed that when the individual reached the point where this kind of total, self-giving love was possible, then a certain (i.e., a *qualified*) type of sinlessness was also possible. The heart captured by God would not be tempted by lesser loves, the mind filled with the thought of God would not be distracted with the inessential, with the banality of evil. The perfect, or "complete," love of God necessarily excludes everything contrary to the goodness God intends for the created order. It is this particular vision of perfection—sinlessness—that has caused so much perplexity and division, both before Wesley and since.

Specifically, the church taught that sanctifying grace effected a real change in the person who had been reborn through conversion and baptism. The working of the Spirit within the individual believer was not simply a revivification but a purgation, a cleansing tongue of fire that destroyed, first, the grossest effects of original sin and, finally—either on this side of the grave or the other—the deepest, stubbornest stains that lay hidden in the farthest reaches of the unconscious. Perfection, like sin, resided in the will. Love, like sin, was not a feeling but a *decision*. Thus the person who had committed herself—heart, soul, mind, and body—to God could be counted on not to commit serious (or deadly) sins as well as deliberate, not deadly but still debilitating sins. Hidden, subconscious sins, personal quirks and imperfections, or mistakes based on igno-

rance were not considered obstacles to perfection as the
church understood it. This type of human frailty was
expected to remain with us until death.

The tendency, for most of us, is to imagine perfection as
a kind of stasis—a final point or plateau, especially if we
think of it in terms of completion or maturity—but this is a
fundamental misunderstanding of what the church means
by perfection. In the first place, scripture and tradition
both assume that we are always moving either toward
God or away from God. We never simply stand still and
tread water, so to speak. (Lukewarmness, you will recall,
puts us outside the pale. Cf. Rev. 3:16.) But if we are
meant to become like a God who is limitless love, then
there can be no limit to our love for God. In that sense, we
are never finished, never complete in having "enough"
love. Perfection in love does not mean having enough
love, nor does it mean having all the love it is possible to
have. Rather, it means *loving to full capacity*—however
small or great that capacity may be. And the issue is not
the size of our capacity. We may be small vessels or large,
elaborately designed or extremely simple. We are
perfected when we are filled to the brim with a yearning
for God. And we cannot be filled to the brim with desire
for God until we are emptied of all lesser loves. As I have
heard it expressed, perfection means not using two talents
when we actually have ten at our disposal.

By the same token, the God whom we must learn to
love to full capacity sets no limits to his love for us. The
unlimited love of God promises to make saints out of the
least promising material: us. Thus the doctrine of
Christian perfection is as optimistic about God as the
doctrine of original sin is pessimistic about human
nature.

The early church fathers, many of whom were imbued

with a platonistic world view or philosophical idealism, found the notion of Christian perfection to be extremely congenial and fruitful. Clement of Alexandria, an important influence on John Wesley, articulated the goal of Christian maturity in terms of an unbroken, continuous contemplation of God. The Beatific Vision, as it is traditionally known, is the final destination of love. It is the perfect union of the lover and the loved: God and the individual identity. All human love relationships tend toward this state of ecstatic union, even when they are deeply flawed by sinful motives and circumstances. We all want, ultimately, to be able to stand outside ourselves—to be freed from the prison of self which separates us from the object we adore. How wonderful then to realize that our faith promises us precisely this experience of total consummation. In the uninterrupted loving gaze of God, we will find all our lost loves, all our unspoken declarations of affection, all our incompleted gropings toward a life-giving intimacy completed. Finished. *Perfected*.

But as one scholar has put it, Clement knew that "the prize of the Christian life is not to be won without dust and heat." Sanctity, like faith, is a gift from God, "yet the reception of that gift is costly to the soul. The price to be paid is prayer."[2] Always, the church has taught that prayer is the path to perfection. Like the Word preached from the pulpit or the Word spoken over the gifts of bread and wine, the words offered and received in conversation with God are efficacious—they can effect real change in the person praying.

The real change that comes about through prayer also changes the way we pray. As in all other areas of life, the life of prayer entails the struggle with self that inevitably accompanies the quest for spiritual maturity. The beginner's prayer asks for things that benefit the self: health, success, deliverance from disaster, a good professional appointment. Those on the way to perfection will ask for the sake of others. When they ask for themselves they will ask most insistently for the gift of perfect love. They will ask God to enable them to love as God loves. Finally, there is only one petition. In the end, one asks for God. Nothing else.

The quest for perfection soon became organized. Around the middle of the third century, an earnest and idealistic young Egyptian heard preached the passage from Matthew in which Jesus tells the young man who would be perfect to "go and sell what you own and give the money to the poor . . . ; then come, follow me" (19:21). Taking this advice to heart, the man, who was only twenty years of age, gave away the land he had inherited and went to live on the desert margin of the village. His goal was to learn to pray without ceasing, and he soon discovered that the fulfillment of this goal required enormous dedication, for evil always vigorously resists the aggressive pursuit of holiness. St. Anthony of Egypt paid a high price for sanctity. Beset with ferocious temptations, he practiced many austerities and ultimately became a spiritual hero to other idealistic young people who came seeking him for guidance and instruction. Thus were born the antecedents of Christian monasticism.

Monasticism, still alive if not entirely well, has always been the preserve of those who have chosen to make the pursuit of Christian perfection a full-time occupation. The attainment of the traditional ideal of perfection as perfect love has been the conscious, governing motive of all the founders of religious orders, and those who joined them did so because they were seeking support for their desire to obey the injunction of the gospel to renounce all for the sake of Christ and to pattern their lives after his example.

Many Christians commonly assume that the monk or nun is a person of near superhuman strength of purpose who, because of that strength, chooses a life of uncommon spiritual hardship. No doubt those who harbor these assumptions would be disconcerted to discover that the monastic life is lived by people who, far from being pillars of strength before entering the monastery, are ordinary people whose hearts and imaginations have been captured by a vision and who, risking all, have thrown themselves entirely on the grace of God.

The people who share this misconception about what is required prior to taking a religious vow would find odd, also, the traditional assumption in monasticism that the practice of the evangelical counsels—poverty, chastity, and obedience—is, in the first place, biblically justifiable, and, in the second, designed to make the quest for perfection easier, not more difficult. The spiritual challenge of married life was originally seen to be greater than that of celibacy. Precisely the opposite is true in today's culture.

The asceticism or discipline we normally associate with monastic spirituality is sometimes, but not often, admired, and almost always misunderstood. The continental reformers tended to see spiritual disciplines as a form of "good works" through which the individual hoped to merit salvation. Human nature being what it is, the danger always exists that even the attempt to restrain the assertive self can become a source of pride and self-satisfaction. The virtue of self-restraint lies always in what motivates it. The ambition for spiritual heroism or the feeding of self-hatred defeat the authentic practice of self-restraint. When we say no to the self, it must be for the purpose of saying yes to God.

The Wesleys, on the other hand, embraced certain ascetical practices and were not at all nervous about whether they might be construed as good works. Like members of monastic orders, they understood these various forms of self-restraint as necessary for an apostolic style of life. Prayer, fasting, almsgiving, constant communion, visiting the sick and imprisoned—all the carefully scheduled practices of the members of the Holy Club—were undertaken for the love of God, for the sake of a love like the love of God.

In early Methodism we have a particularly apt example of how the spirit of the evangelical counsels can inform the attitudes and spiritual practices of ordinary people. The communal accountability that worked so successfully in monastic orders functioned with similar effectiveness through the class meeting and band structures John Wesley initiated with his followers. This form of small-group spiritual formation was an ingenious response to the needs of laypersons who, like members of religious orders, wanted to take Christ's invitation to perfection seriously. The special effectiveness of these structures lay in their faithfulness to the tradition which claims that all baptized Christians are part of one new Being, the Body of Christ. If we believe this, then we cannot argue—as so many Americans today would—that our stance before God is a private affair. Similarly, the nuclear family is, or can be, an intentional Christian community in which self-restraint and selfless love may be practiced on a daily basis. But the church has a long way to go before this fundamental insight can be appreciated by the majority of Christians.

I don't wish to leave the impression that it will be relatively easy to recover an authentic ascetical practice as an essential element of a classical or Wesleyan spirituality. As you might imagine, it is more than a matter of "just saying no." What looks initially like a battle between raw human will and overpowering temptation must eventually be understood as yet another divine initiative in our lives—an invitation to trust God's grace rather than our own strength of character. It is a bit like having to wade deeply into the sea before the waters actually part, but as one writer puts it:

> The bird bears its wings, but still more the wings support the bird. In like manner, the religious virtues and the three vows impose special obligations, it is true; but above all, they bear souls toward the perfection of charity [love] over a more rapid and sure road.[3]

Thomas a Kempis says the same thing even more forcefully: "Carry the cross patiently and with perfect submission, and in the end, it shall carry you."

Perfection as an Objective, Countercultural Norm

As we have seen, the ideal of perfection continued to be a vital spiritual norm for Christians in the centuries that followed the church of the New Testament. But the Christian ideal of perfection was not the only such ideal competing for the individual Christian's loyalty. A common cultural ideal in unconverted Europe was that of *fortitude*. The perfect human being was physically brave and could be counted on to resist the enemy at all costs, even to the point of death. This same cultural value tended to exalt the exceptionally dangerous or risky undertaking.

Typically, perfection of this sort was embedded in and contributed to a strong sense of national pride. Christians living during the time of the Roman Empire were expected to resist this value. They understood that the lordship of Caesar was antithetical to the lordship of Christ, that they were sojourners here, living in exile from their spiritual home.

If a crucified messiah was essentially an embarrassment in classical antiquity, it is no less of a problem today. This most central of all our religious symbols does not suggest heroic resistance. Nevertheless, fortitude, as a pervasive cultural ideal, did influence the spiritual life of the church. In the earliest centuries, the church experienced many martyrdoms—a tragic reality that came to acquire a certain triumphalist connotation in a setting where heroic resistance was valued so highly. In later centuries, when martyrdom was much less frequent, extreme forms of asceticism echoed this same value when, instead of being seen as means to an end, they became ends in themselves. What the church has always maintained is that the value of martyrdom and asceticism lies in the love that motivates them and not in the courage or sheer force of will that may be needed to sustain them.

Modern American secular culture continues to promote this value when it applauds the rugged individualist who battles against all odds to follow her own particular star, when it grossly overpays its modern-day gladiators for making it to the Super Bowl, and when it "stands tall" for democracy against Communist aggression in Third World countries while at the same time practicing a studied indifference to the plight of countless human beings who lack the fundamental necessities of food, shelter, basic education, and medical care.

Ancient cultures infused with Greek and Roman values also had another ideal of perfection: the ideal of wisdom. For the philosophers, the intellect is what distinguishes human life from other, less complex forms of life. They argued, therefore, that the perfection of humankind lies in the perfection of this unique faculty: reason. Failing to take account of the quirkiness of free will, they assumed that once human beings *knew* the good, they would inevitably pursue it and so act as to bring it about.

As the church encountered and began to appropriate classical culture in various ways, it came smack-up against this rationalistic ideal that equated brains with moral virtue and spiritual aptitude. When elements in the church succumbed to this cultural value, the result was gnosticism—the great temptation of the intellectual Christian. If we can just find the "secret sayings of Jesus," if we can just get beyond the superstitious beliefs and practices of popular religion, if we can just apply the correct exegetical techniques and a demythologizing hermeneutic to this passage, *then* we shall be privy to the Truth—the Truth that makes us free.

The gnostic Christian is always the Christian who "knows better"—who has risen above the *hoi polloi* and has privileged access to information that the common person cannot be expected to understand. Modern American secular culture continues to exalt this value in

its obsession with technique and technology, its
rapacious domination of the natural order, and its
steadfast rationalistic rejection of the supernatural.

It is perhaps discouraging to see how little things
change. The Christian ideal of perfection as crucified
Love receives no serious cultural recognition or
ratification now, nor did it when the church was new.
On the other hand, it should be encouraging to
recognize that the early church did find the moral and
spiritual resources to resist dominant cultural values
which, though good in themselves, subvert Christian
faith when they are given pride of place in our lives.

It is commonplace for each generation to decide that
never before in human history have the forces of good
been so heavily besieged by the forces of evil. It is
another instance of inordinate pride, I think, that
makes us want to believe that our crises are the worst
ever, that faith is much more difficult now than it used
to be—before Kant, Freud, Einstein, and the atom
bomb. I am not a historian, but I have had good history
teachers, and I know enough to know that things have
almost always looked bad. Faith is never easy, and
culture consistently finds ways to subvert the gospel.

One of the things I most admire in Wesley was his
willingness to challenge the high culture of his day—of
which he himself was a product—for the sake of making
the gospel available to those for whom that culture was
an insurmountable barrier to a vital piety. He was not
afraid to look religiously ridiculous in the eyes of his
peers—to be filled to the brim with an intoxicating love
that others sneeringly labeled "enthusiasm."

I admire, too, Wesley's refusal to be tied entirely to
his own time and theological tradition. Wesley's mind
was open, absorbent, argumentative, and he eagerly

CHRISTIAN PERFECTION IN CHRISTIAN TRADITION   *39*

looked to scriptural, patristic, medieval, and Reformation sources for whatever truth they might have to offer. Unlike so many Christians today, he did not believe that things must be current to be relevant. The world might be changing, but the God who is Truth can be trusted to speak plainly in every age, and we are foolish indeed if we think the whole truth lies in what has been published in the second half of the twentieth century.

Finally, I must confess to feeling a deep kinship with the young Wesley, who wanted so badly to be "perfect." I sympathize with the elaborate schemes and schedules he concocted as a hedge against spiritual lassitude. He loved no solution more, I think, than a "program." Of course, he had to learn—by means of failed programs—that the work of perfecting himself was beyond him. He could not control God's agenda by deciding if, when, or how. The actual experience of spiritual surrender is not something any one of us can simply decide to have. Mostly, we are driven to it when all our personal resources—our high-minded ideals, our plans, our programs for spiritual self-improvement— have come to naught.

Our unceasing prayers, our well-meaning attempts at self-restraint, our repeated efforts to serve the neighbor, are not what do the "perfecting." What they do in fact accomplish is to prepare us for perfection by *emptying* us, and this is the reason these practices are so essential. But it is the Spirit of God, the Spirit of Holiness, that perfects us by filling us full to the brim, full to overflowing with the love that loves like God. An older and wiser John Wesley understood this, and what is more, he expected it to happen.

~ ~ ~

I went begging from door to door on the village road
when your golden chariot appeared in the distance, like
a splendid dream, and I wondered who was this king of
all kings!

My hopes increased, and I thought, "The bad days are
over," and I was ready in the hope of spontaneous alms
and riches scattered everywhere in the dust.

The chariot stopped where I was standing. Your
glance fell upon me and you got down smiling. I felt that
the great moment of my life had finally come. Then,
suddenly, you extended your right hand and said:
"What do you have to give me?"

What royal game was this, extending your hand to a
beggar in order to beg! I was confused and remained
perplexed. Finally, from my sack, I slowly drew a small
grain of wheat and gave it to you.

But how great was my surprise when at the end of the
day I emptied my sack and found a small grain of gold
amid the pile of meager grains. I wept bitterly, and then
thought, "Why didn't I have the heart to give you my
whole self?"

—Bernard Bro[4]

DISCUSSION QUESTIONS

1. In what ways have we been captured by the
dominant cultural values of personal excellence and
self-fulfillment in the seminary or local church? In
particular, how have these values affected our understanding of the meaning of salvation?
2. What is it in us that prefers the model of discovery in
spiritual growth and resists that of formation or shaping?
Again, what does this suggest about our doctrine of
salvation?

3. What are the things in our lives that are analogous to the "possessions" of the rich young man in Luke? What strategies do we employ to "cushion" our existence against the kind of nakedness and vulnerability that Christian perfection requires?

4. To what extent does the vision of sanctity, that is, of a real change as opposed to a forensic (imputed) change in our status before God, engage you? Are you satisfied, as Luther seemed to be, simply to be forgiven, or would you, like Wesley, welcome the kind of radical transformation that holiness implies?

NOTES

1. George Lindbeck, "Spiritual Formation and Theological Formation," *Theological Education*, suppl. 1, 1988, vol. 24, pp. 17-18: "Something like spiritual therapy can have a place, not only in initial but also in later stages of formation. Difficulties become insuperable only when the therapeutic approach is taken as normative, when a model of what might be called 'exfoliation' replaces 'formation.' When this happens the spiritual life is seen as one of discovering and creatively expressing a pre-given individual identity, and no attention is payed to that internalization of a communal religious tradition which is the condition for fruitful spiritual self-expression or exfoliation, for authentic individuality and genuine creativity. When the development of spiritual selfhood is well advanced, the process of self-discovery can be an integral part of maturation, but not before. Meister Eckhart's search for the spark within or the Quaker turn towards the inner light did not take place without formation."
2. R. Newton Flew, *The Idea of Perfection in Christian Theology* (London: Humphrey Milford and Oxford University Press, 1934), p. 143.
3. Réginald Garrigou-Lagrange, O.P., *The Three Ages of the Interior Life* (St. Louis and London: B. Herder Book Co., 1949), p. 212.
4. Bernard Bro, O.P., *Learning to Pray*, trans. John Morriss (Staten Island, N.Y.: Alba House, 1966), p. 150.

2

The Love of God
and the Life of Prayer

*Hear, O Israel: The Lord our God is one
Lord; and you shall love the Lord your God
with all your heart, and with all your soul,
and with all your might.* (Deut. 6:4-5 RSV)

Almost everyone has (at least once) fallen madly, passionately in love. Take a moment to think back over that experience. Try to recall the way in which it simply "took over" your life. Suddenly, everything seemed different—everything you saw, heard, tasted, or felt was touched by a kind of magical intensity. The thought of your beloved never entirely left you. Even when forced to concentrate on some necessary task, you found that image always hovering on the borders of consciousness, lending a kind of amazement and zest to things that would otherwise seem routine or difficult. That one, wonderful love not only changed the meaning of every act you performed, it changed the meaning of who you were by challenging your previous sense of yourself. Suddenly, *you* were wonderful too—and not because you deserved it. You were wonderful simply because someone wonderful thought and said so. Wandering around with an idiotic grin on your face, you were also slightly insane.

That kind of transforming love is necessarily all-

encompassing and exclusive. Each fiber of our being is
caught up in the experience. Our every waking thought
awaits the next encounter with the beloved. Everything
that happens to us, significant or paltry, must be shared.
Unable to help ourselves, we are driven by a need to
unite in every conceivable way with the object of our
devotion. We want to "step out" of ourselves and
become lost in the act of union. We want, quite literally,
to *become* what we love.

Of course, we fail. What we love always remains
tantalizingly out of reach—no matter how close we get,
no matter how hard we try. There is always an
"otherness" that remains utterly impenetrable. There is
a longing in us, a thirst that somehow never gets
completely quenched. So when one relationship fails us,
we move on to another thinking that *this* time things will
be different—that the problem resided in the personal
failings of the other, if not in ourselves. When we find
the "right" person, things will be perfect.

That our human cravings for love are never fully
satisfied does not change the reality that we become
what we love. The human psyche slowly but surely
wraps itself around what it loves, assuming the identical
contours, whatever they may be. We have all seen older
married couples who have grown somehow to look alike,
who can anticipate each other's responses, who
complete each other's sentences. Years of loving have
produced a comfortable complementarity. Devoted
mates grow into a kind of mutual fitness for one another.
By the same token, we have seen people whose
alienating love for less worthy objects—money, professional success, sexual adventure, alcohol—has visibly
transformed them. We can see the hard lines of
ambition, the creases of lust and dissipation etched into

the faces of those who have become complicit in their own destruction.

Those who love completely do become what they love. The problem we face today is that few people are ready to risk themselves in an exclusive love relationship. Today's clergy can probably count on the fingers of one hand the number of couples who have come to them recently for premarital counseling who have not already decided to live together first. Fewer and fewer people are ready to risk the total commitment that a healthy marriage requires without doing an extended "test drive." And, once married, many persons who think of themselves as good Christians believe that they have the right to engage in additional intimate relationships and that these other experiences do not constitute marital infidelity. The claim here is that love does not need to be exclusive; we can give to others without necessarily taking anything away from our spouse.

Scripture, of course, says otherwise. The great commandment of both the Old and the New Testament is that the one great Love which is paradigmatic for all our lesser loves must be an *exclusive* love: "Hear, O Israel: The Lord our God is one Lord; and you shall love the Lord your God with all your heart, and with all your soul, and with all your might" (Deut. 6:4-5 RSV). Yahweh, we are told, is a jealous God who will not share our devotion with some other worthy person or object. God wants it all—*all* our heart, *all* our soul, *all* our might, and, in Luke's version, *all* our mind.

How would we react to anyone or anything else who made this kind of claim on us? Eagerly? Probably not. Most likely we would be very suspicious, very wary, very hesitant. And rightly so. Only someone head-over-heels in love would be likely to say yes to such a possibility—and we know that such people are a little bit crazy!

The next question is tougher: How do we react when it is God who is doing the asking? Are we any more eager or responsive? Almost certainly not. Yet that is what we are commanded to do, not invited, but commanded. Who or what can command our love? Who can dare say I want you to love me—only me—to want me and nothing but me? Isn't it the case that God only wants us to love God first, or most? Isn't there supposed to be plenty of love left to go around?

Let us leave aside for the moment these troubling questions about God's justification for making this demand and concentrate instead on the general condition of mild craziness—of "in loveness"—that might predispose us to say yes to the possibility of total commitment. What is it that creates the conditions whereby two persons can even imagine this kind of whole-hearted, whole-souled, and physically exclusive relationship?

What usually captures us mentally and emotionally is the quality of attractiveness. Something beautiful beckons us into relationship. It may be physical beauty; it may be beauty of soul. Whatever it is, when it calls to us it is compelling, and because we have been made to love the beautiful, the good, and the true, we want to respond.

There is always a certain risk involved in responding. We are afraid of personal rejection in the first place and of disappointed hopes and disillusionment in the second. The relationship may not work. If we fear failure more than we desire love, we will not take the risk—or we will ask for a "test drive" and, like a customer of a used-car dealer, start thinking about driving a hard bargain.

If we are willing to take the risk, then we must be prepared to invest ourselves ever-increasingly as the relationship progresses along a course that is alternately pleasurable and painful. We begin by getting acquainted, by sharing some of the externals of our lives: Who are you? This is who I am. We continue by sharing some of our interior lives: This is what I think; what do you think? Eventually, if what has attracted us in the first place is not only beautiful but true, then we begin to share what we feel. This is what I love; this is what I fear. What do you love? What do you fear?

The course of a genuine love relationship takes the form of a progressively risky emotional "stripping" in which we allow ourselves to become increasingly vulnerable to the other. The stripping must take place if we are to be fully known—something for which each one of us yearns. Physical nakedness can be a symbol of that vulnerability but not always. The full surrender that comes with the revelation of emotional nakedness is a very rare and powerful event in the lives of any two lovers. Yet without that surrender, no real union is possible.

More than anything else, understanding what it means to be "in love" has helped me to see what God requires of me. The command to love God with all our heart, all our soul, all our strength, and all our mind is really an invitation to fall in love, to engage one-on-one in a personal sharing that is nothing less than a severe emotional stripping. And like any love affair, it will be ardent and arduous both.

The divine invitation to an unreserved or perfect love requires an object that is infinitely attractive. In this case, too, we must be beckoned into relationship by something or Someone. God, the Great I Am, comes

looking for me, a little "would be," in a shape I can
recognize—in the shape of *human* being. True God from
True God—irresistibly attractive in the man Jesus of
Nazareth—beckons us into the ultimate love relationship.

The risks are evident from the beginning. We know
this beckoning is to an exclusive commitment. We know
we will not have any bargaining power in this
arrangement. The terms of the relationship are already
determined—and not by us. We will not be the ones to
decide how close we want to get; we will not be
permitted to keep God at a manageable distance, so that
the exchange between us will always be "civil" or polite.
Written into the relationship is the commitment to that
delicate yet relentless, exquisitely painful stripping
process.

To respond to that irresistibly attractive and exclusive
beckoning, we must let go all other attachments—all
those possessions that in actuality possess us—all our
personal hopes, dreams, ambitions, and loves; and we
must exchange them for Christ's—*his* hopes, dreams,
ambitions, and loves. For that is what union with God is
all about—to be so hopelessly in love that nothing will
satisfy our desires unless it first satisfies the One we
love.

But let us say, for the sake of our argument, that you
are willing to take this risk, that you want to know this
man, Jesus—God's beckoning to us—and belong to him
in an intimate love relationship. What does this mean? It
means, first, that you must invest yourself and your time
in nurturing that relationship, just as you would for any
other important relationship in your life. Implicit in the
command to love God with all our resources and to full

capacity, is the apostolic exhortation to pray without ceasing.

Prayer is the essence of and the structure for an intimate, I-Thou relationship with God. It is the means by which mutual sharing can gradually increase. Just as it makes no sense to tell someone, "I love you more than anything in the world, but I just can't manage to find the time to be with you," it makes no sense to claim that we have no time for prayer. When we love someone we naturally want to spend time together; and when we are "in love" with someone, we *make* the time to be with our beloved. That shared time is essential, for without it we cannot possibly come to know each other. It takes time, private time, in which to reveal our thoughts, our feelings, our hopes, dreams, fears, our joys and sorrows, ourself. In the busy lives of dual-career couples, coordinating calendars for the sake of private time together can be extremely difficult. In the case of our relationship to God, it is much easier. There is only one calendar to consult: ours. The infinitely attractive One who beckons us into relationship is always there, instantly available.

The life of prayer begins in a deceptively simple way. It begins with a commitment to make time for the relationship—to show up for our appointment. I say "deceptively simple" because most of us know how terribly difficult this first step is. In fact, the only step likely to be more difficult than the first, is the last, and that is so far down the road we cannot even be sure of what it is.

For most of us, the divine-human exchange begins with a form of polite and civil discourse. We say "please" and "thank you" and "would it be all right if." We are concerned about being "good," or if not good, then at least theologically correct. Often we engage in second-guessing God: "God is not concerned with trivial issues; therefore, this is not appropriate matter for prayer." "My personal desires are not the point; it's clear that God's purposes are at stake here." If you are anything like me, you want to be strong, unselfish, and lofty in your prayer life. But the need to be good or correct or, at least, not trivial or silly is ultimately an obstacle to intimacy with God.

Any relationship that skirts areas of possible tension or emotional difficulty will never ripen into deep friendship or love. Eventually our prayer must go beyond the conventional niceties of acquaintanceship to emotional truthfulness. This is never so easy as it sounds. In my own case, my need to be "strong," "correct," and "not silly" in my relationship to God lasted for a period of many years. About one issue in particular, I felt I had to keep a stiff upper lip, spiritually speaking, because I was sure I knew what God's will for me must be—and it was not what I wanted. Yet I was so determined to "accept God's will" and carry on in difficult circumstances that I could not admit, even to myself, that this was not what I wanted. It was only after much mental and emotional suffering that I was able to wring the truth from myself and admit to God that I was licked. In that moment of truth, the basis for the relationship shifted just as the ground shifts in an earthquake, and I was the recipient of a great and terrible grace: God gave me what I wanted.

I had not wanted to see that side of myself, and I had not wanted God to see it either. But without that emotional stripping, no intimacy, no progress is possible. I hope I have learned that lesson well, but I don't imagine that will make the self-revelation lying ahead any easier. In my case, the process has just begun after a ridiculously long period of preliminaries.

On the other hand, one thing has become easier. With the increase in truthfulness and intimacy in my relationship with God, it is no longer so difficult to find private time to invest in that relationship. I find myself rising earlier with less effort and more enthusiasm; I find myself craving communion; and I find myself anticipating my next "appointment" with pleasure throughout the day. To be frank, it is not so different from being "in love." The beckoning image of the Savior now hovers most of the time on the horizon of consciousness, and the more my hunger for God is fed by prayer, the hungrier I become.

Then what? Gradually, our need to unburden and to reveal ourselves before God gives way to another need: the need simply to *be together*. To pray without ceasing does not mean to talk without ceasing. It means to place oneself constantly in the presence of God—to listen as much as to speak, or simply to gaze on the object of one's affection. Think back again to what it means to be enamored of someone. Eventually, there is no need to fill the moments with words. We simply sit and stare, like a pair of besotted idiots. All we want is to *look* at what we love. And it is at this point that something very important in the spiritual life begins to happen.

The self-stripping that inevitably occurs when we are faithful in prayer pares us down to size. We become very small, very dependent. As our own insignificance begins to dawn on us, we find we are less protective of ourselves and more concerned to love that which loves us. For that is where our significance lies—in loving and in being loved. When the object of our attention and concern shifts from ourselves and our needs to that of the concerns and needs of the one we love, a corner has been turned. At this point our own petitions are no longer central—they are not in fact what our prayer is about. Eventually, our prayer is about God, not us. What we come to focus on is the object of our affection: Jesus Christ. When we are concentrating on *our* needs, *our* problems—even *our* love—we are still thinking about us, not God.

As our gaze shifts and our own insignificance is accepted, we begin to see just what or Whom it is we love, and in loving God—most particularly God in the shape of "human" being—that psychic wrapping process begins. The object upon which our loving gaze rests begins to reshape us, ever so gradually, around its own contours. We begin to become what we love. To the extent that we are conscious of *what* we love, and not how much *we* love, that reshaping will proceed with less resistance on our part.

This process is what John Wesley and the Western tradition refer to as "sanctification." Eastern Orthodoxy calls it "divinization"; I have also heard it referred to as "christification." Whichever term is used, each one suggests a radical change in the person, and this change is what the relationship is all about, it is what we are beckoned to, for without it, the union we so long for can never occur.

It is important for us to remember that it is not simply we who yearn for that union. The God who made us yearns for it even more, and that unimaginably strong and perpetual divine longing is what accounts for the Incarnation. God come in the shape of human being is, according to St. Catherine of Siena, God "crazy in love" with human beings. By assuming our limitations—by becoming *like us*—say the early church fathers, God made it possible for us to become *like God,* and so this most amazing, divinely initiated exchange is what makes our union with God possible. God became what God loved.

This great act of divine condescension is not simply what makes prayer efficacious; it is what makes prayer possible at all. Many of us get discouraged in our efforts to pray. We are easily distracted and impatient for results. When the high standards we set for ourselves are not met, we feel like giving up in disgust. Our repeated failures should alert us to a fundamental misunderstanding on our part. When God became what God loved it was not simply for a span of some thirty-odd years. The divine commitment to dealing with our limitations persists just as the divine desire for union with us persists. And that commitment condescends even to praying on our behalf.

Paul makes reference to this divine commitment when he says,

> The Spirit too comes to help us in our weakness. For when we cannot choose words in order to pray properly, the Spirit . . . expresses our plea in a way that could never be put into words, and God who knows everything in our hearts knows perfectly well what [the Spirit] means, and that the pleas of the saints expressed by the Spirit are according to the mind of God.
>
> (Rom. 8:26-27)

Now this is a truly amazing thing! So eager is our Creator for union with us that God is willing to pray *in our stead.* The prayers prayed in us by the Spirit are "according to the mind of God." This means they are prayed in union with God. Most of what we normally call "prayer" is really a kind of preparation for the Spirit to begin to move in us. The showing up for our appointment, the silence, the effort to center ourselves, the use of a scriptural text or some other form of spiritual reading is all a kind of beckoning on our part to the Spirit. Understanding this lifts a great burden from our shoulders. Our inability to pray well is not simply a personal failure on our parts, it is a failure of the human condition itself. But God takes our weakness into account and prays in our place.

Once we understand this, many things which at first look impossible become real possibilities. Take the notion of praying without ceasing. None of us is able to devote every waking minute to conscious prayer; we need to buy groceries, pay bills, enjoy the company of friends, and earn a living. But we can invite the Spirit to pray in us at all times and trust that this indeed is happening. One of the things I have learned to do recently, just before I turn out the lights at night, is to ask the Spirit to pray constantly in me while I sleep.

Similarly, the terribly vexing demand of Christian perfection that we pray for our enemies requires, I believe, an absolute reliance on the work of the Spirit in us. Our wounded pride, our fear, our grudging resentment—these things taint our prayers. But God, "who knows everything in our hearts knows perfectly well what [the Spirit] means," and our imperfect pleas for our enemies, purified in the groanings of the Spirit, are, in spite of our weaknesses, "according to the mind of God."

Now, if the real work of praying is done in us through the Spirit, does this mean our efforts to pray effectively through some sort of disciplined method are in vain? Certainly not. The beckoning on our part is essential to the growth of a relationship of mutual love between us and the Lord, and as the relationship begins to mature, our willingness to undertake various prayer disciplines will increase.

How do we know when the Spirit is praying in us? I don't think we always can; maybe we mostly can't. It is certainly not simply a reference to speaking in tongues. I suspect what the Spirit has to say on our behalf really cannot be uttered in *any* tongue. But there are times, during and after prayer, when we are aware of a power, an energy that somehow carries us or speaks to us or quiets us or refreshes us. These wonderful experiences the tradition calls "consolations." They are gifts, and they bring with them a degree of reassurance that something is going on somewhere.

Does that then mean that when we don't feel anything at all nothing is happening? Is it worthwhile to continue praying when we don't feel we are getting anything out of it? That's really the same as asking, "Is it worthwhile staying married now that the glow, the romance has faded?" We know that the point of married life is a great deal more than romance. The same holds true in our relationship with God. We do not show up for our appointment simply because we expect to get something good out of the experience, just as we do not go home at night to our spouses simply because we expect them to do something good for us. We go home to them because we are *married* to them. And we spend time in prayer because we *belong to God.* Just as an unspoken, undemonstrated love may exist for long periods of time, so we must also assume that the Spirit continues to pray in our stead, even when we are not conscious of anything good—or of anything at all—happening. Just as there have been times in our lives when God has beckoned to us over and over again, and we have not responded, so there may be times in our lives when it seems that we are beckoning into the void. Let us learn to be as patient with God as God has been patient with us.

"You must therefore be perfect just as your heavenly Father is perfect" (Matt. 5:48). Become what you love, and you will love what God loves. Love the just, the unjust, the righteous, the criminal, the wealthy, the poor, the friend, the enemy. Perfect love loves that which deserves no love. And God, the perfect Lover, is crazy in love with all of us.

~ ~ ~

Why then,
Eternal Father,
did you create this creature of yours?
I am truly amazed at this,
and indeed I see,
as you show me,
that you made us for one reason only:
in your light
you saw yourself compelled
by the fire of your charity
to give us being,
in spite of the evil we would commit against you,
Eternal Father.
It was fire, then,
that compelled you.
O unutterable love,
even though you saw all the evils
that all your creatures would commit
against your infinite goodness,
you acted as if you did not see

and set your eye
only on the beauty of your creature,
with whom you had fallen in love
like one drunk and crazy with love.
And in love you drew us out of yourself,
giving us being
in your own image and likeness.
You, eternal Truth,
have told me the truth:
that love compelled you to create us.
Even though you saw that we would offend you,
your charity would not let you set your eyes on
that sight.
No,
You took your eyes off the sin that was to be
and fixed your gaze
only on your creature's beauty.
For if you had concentrated on the sin,
you would have forgotten the love you had
for creating humankind.
Not that the sin was hid from you,
but you concentrated on the love
because you are nothing but a fire of love,
crazy over what you have made.
But give me the grace, dearest love,
that my body may give up its blood
for the honor and glory of your name.
Let me no longer be clothed in myself.

—Catherine of Siena[1]

DISCUSSION QUESTIONS

1. How helpful or disconcerting is it to compare your prayer life with the human experience of falling in love?

What new insights does it produce? What specific
challenges does it raise?
2. How would you characterize your discourse with
God in prayer? Is it relatively formal, or intimate? What
standards of appropriateness do you typically apply to
this exchange?
3. What difference does, or might, it make to our prayer
life to begin to think in terms of the Spirit praying in us
on our behalf?

NOTE

1. Reprinted from *The Prayers of Catherine of Siena*, trans. Suzanne Noffke,
   O.P. (New York: Paulist Press, 1983), pp. 112-13. © 1983 by Suzanne
   Noffke, O.P. Used by permission of Paulist Press.

— 3 —

The Love of God
and the Love of Neighbor

*I tell you solemnly, in so far as you did this to
one of the least of these . . . , you did it to
me.*   (Matt. 25:40)

One of the oddities of human love is the way in which it
enlarges us. The freely given love of another person gives
birth to something in us that cannot be contained within the
parameters of the self—something that bursts precipitously
through the barriers we have erected to protect ourselves
from disappointment and humiliation. The one unmistak-
able sign of a love that is true is the impulse it creates toward
generosity, magnanimity, the willingness to give others the
benefit of the doubt.

We have spoken of how being in love is a form of
re-creation, of how we become what we love. This
transformation of the one who loves occurs—in spite of
the sometimes stubborn resistance to love lodged in
fallen human nature—because we have been made to
love, by Love, in the image and likeness of Love. And if
the first effect of the arrival of love in our lives is to give
us an entirely new image of ourselves (we must be
wonderful, because someone wonderful loves us), then
the second effect follows necessarily: Suddenly the rest
of the world looks wonderful too. If at first nothing

matters but the loved, eventually we discover the scope of our love expanding to include that which the beloved loves.

The enlargement or expansiveness of the self who loves is most evident in this taking on, this assumption, of the loves of the beloved. Take the very simple example of the bookish, unathletic adolescent girl who suddenly develops a taste for football or track because that is what is important to her boyfriend. Nothing but love can account for it! Or consider the man who, for love of a widow, unselfishly assumes the burden of raising—and loving—her children by the deceased spouse. "Love me, love my children," she says; and he does. The children this man finds himself father to may or may not be lovable. Yet he loves them even when they are rude, hostile, and ungrateful for the support he supplies—not because they are really "good kids," or needy and deserving, but because they are *hers*. And he loves them by providing for their legitimate human needs, treating them with patience and respect, and supplying affection and discipline both, especially when these things are least welcome.

The idea of perfection in Christian tradition assumes this epiphenomenon of love, this enlargement of soul. Perfect love is, in the first place, the whole-souled love of God, our Maker: "You shall love the Lord your God with all your heart, and with all your soul, and with all your strength, and with all your mind . . . " But it is not "perfect" until the love fills us to the brim and then brims over: "and your neighbor as yourself" (Luke 10:27 RSV). The love of God, in which we become *like God*, entails loving what God loves, and what God loves is the world.

The command to love the neighbor is taken with great seriousness in the church's spiritual tradition. Countless good works have been performed in obedience to it. Some Christians have taken it much more seriously than others. Particular traditions, including that which goes by the name "Wesleyan," have definitively identified themselves by their adherence to this teaching, though not without persistent and troubling conflicts about how the command is to be interpreted. But since the commandment to love the neighbor as we love ourselves is essential to what is meant by Christian perfection, we cannot afford to be complacent about such divisions and conflicts.

Let us begin by establishing what the command does *not* mean. American culture in the late twentieth century is saturated with psychological categories and therapeutic values. Many priests and ministers who also serve as pastoral counselors are irresistibly drawn toward psychotherapeutic readings of biblical texts. This is understandable but unfortunate. The biblical writers themselves do not "psychologize." For the most part, they do not tell us what the biblical characters are thinking or feeling; they tell us what they *do*. The psychology of Jews in first-century Palestine might be similar on some counts to that of twentieth-century Americans, but the chances are good that there would be some very significant differences. Thus we are on shaky ground when we give these texts a peculiarly psychological reading; yet how many times have we heard Luke 10:27 preached in terms of what it means to "love ourselves"! Over and over again we laypersons have heard preachers insist that we can never really love someone else until we first learn to love ourselves. Such sermonizing deftly turns our attention away from the neighbor by refocusing attention on our wounded psyches. Thus the command to love the neighbor, more often than not, becomes a command to love *ourselves*, a divinely sanctioned call to enhanced self-esteem.

When Jesus answers the scribe's question about how to inherit eternal life, he does so by citing two separate passages from the Hebrew scriptures. The first is the "great" commandment, the *Shema* (Deut. 6:4-5); the second is a passage in Leviticus, which explains, clearly and concretely, what it means to love the neighbor:

> You must not steal nor deal deceitfully or fraudulently with your neighbor. . . . You must not exploit or rob your neighbor. You must not keep back the laborer's wage until next morning. You must not curse the dumb, nor put an obstacle in the blind man's way, but you must fear your God. I am Yahweh.
>
> You must not be guilty of unjust verdicts. You must neither be partial to the little man nor overawed by the great; you must pass judgment on your neighbor according to justice. You must not slander your own people, and you must not jeopardize your neighbor's life. I am Yahweh. You must not bear hatred for your brother in your heart. You must openly tell him, your neighbor, of his offense; this way you will not take a sin upon yourself. You must not exact vengeance, nor must you bear a grudge against the children of your people. You must love your neighbor as yourself. I am Yahweh.   (19:11-18)

Whatever our own particular neuroses may be, they are no obstacle to this kind of "love." The command of Yahweh is simple justice for the neighbor and compassion for the vulnerable. It has nothing to do with personal affection—which is how the modern American understands the word *love*. We are not commanded to feel affection or to be skillful with interpersonal relationships, but we are commanded not to harbor resentment: We must speak "openly" to our neighbor when we or God's law has been offended. The message of the text is plain. We must treat other people as we would want them to treat us—with equity, dignity, patience, and respect.

The term "neighbor" in the Hebrew scriptures most often refers to a fellow Israelite, as it clearly does in this passage, but the fundamental ethos of equity and mutual respect that characterized the relationship between members of the covenant community had a spill-over effect on how Israel was expected to treat the "stranger," that is, the resident alien: "If a stranger lives with you in your land, do not molest him. You must count him as one of your own countrymen and love him as yourself—for you were once strangers yourselves in Egypt. I am Yahweh your God" (Lev. 19:33-34). Having been loved by Yahweh when she was most vulnerable, Israel can well afford to enlarge the borders of her heart and graciously receive the exile. Having been delivered from slavery herself—through no power and by no merit of her own—she cannot afford not to. Even the "enemy" is allowed to profit from the enlargement of Israel's heart: "If you come on your enemy's ox or donkey going astray, you must lead it back to him. If you see the donkey of a man who hates you fallen under its load, instead of keeping out of his way, go to him to help him" (Exod. 23:4-5).

But the line is drawn somewhere. For Israel a limit is set to love. Moses and the "mixed multitude" had sustained an unforgivable lapse of Middle Eastern hospitality while on the march. Thus no Moabite or Ammonite was ever to be allowed into the assembly of Yahweh, not even a tenth-generation descendant:

> Because they did not come to meet you with bread and
> water when you were on your way out of Egypt, and
> because they hired Balaam . . . to curse you. But
> Yahweh your God refused to listen to Balaam, and . . .
> turned the curse into a blessing for you, because
> Yahweh your God loved you. Never, as long as you live,
> shall you seek their welfare or their prosperity.
>
> (Deut. 23:3-6)

Since refusing to offer hospitality in primitive societies
or in desert conditions could be tantamount to a death
sentence, this Israel could neither forget nor forgive.

The answer Jesus elicited from the scribe, by
referring him to scripture, of course did not satisfy. Love
of God and neighbor was nothing new. It was all too
simple. Since the scribe's motives were almost certainly
devious, he pressed the case further: "And who is my
neighbor?" In response, Jesus proceeded to exegete
Leviticus 19:18 by telling a story that was bound to make
the scribe feel extremely uncomfortable, since it
implied yet a further—and most unacceptable—"enlargement" of Israel's heart. It was a story about
hospitality.

The parable of the Good Samaritan (Luke 10:29-37) is
a favorite with many Christians but is widely misunderstood as being simply an injunction to help persons in
need. It is at least that, but like so many of Jesus'
teachings, it has lodged within it something deeply
offensive to human pride. The failure of the priest and
Levite—the community's strongest symbols of sanctity
and religious commitment—to offer assistance to the
wounded traveler is a stinging rebuke to the scribe who
worked in support of the religious establishment. And,

on the other hand, the neighborliness of the despised "foreigner," the Samaritan, is a shocking insult. It is another of those ironic, emotionally impossible reversals that characterized Jesus' preaching. Here again is a flagrant refusal of life's necessities in a life-and-death situation. Here Israel neglects to care for her own in the most rudimentary fashion, and the "unclean," religiously syncretistic Samaritan becomes the bearer of God's grace. Israel's image of herself as the bearer of grace, the "light to the nations," is badly battered by this parable. She who has privileged access to the Truth is ministered to by a heretic.

The remarkable thing about Jesus' preaching is that it never negates *Torah* (or the "Teaching") but always pushes the tradition to expand or enlarge its implications and in so doing requires a painful expansion of us. "You have learned how it was said to our ancestors . . . . But I say this to you" (Matt. 5:21-22). We must love our neighbor as ourselves, but we have not truly understood *who* that neighbor is or what loving the neighbor will cost us.

Our natural response to the command to love our neighbor as ourselves is to equate it with the universal humanitarian impulse to alleviate suffering. It is not necessary to attach any particular religious significance to this impulse. We see it everywhere, among believers, agnostics, and atheists. Yet *Torah* assigns a soteriological or "saving" signification to our acts of charity and justice. The Israelite was to love the neighbor—the fellow Israelite God had graciously deigned to deliver from slavery, and the alien—because Israel too had once been in exile and through no merit of her own had been delivered. To love what God loves is a way of remembering that we have been loved.

The reality of the Incarnation as it came to be understood by the church in no way negates the Hebrew understanding of what it means to love the neighbor. For the Christian, as for the Jew, acts of charity and justice are not simply expressions of the humanitarian impulse but *acts of worship,* ways of remembering; yet in the teaching of Jesus the Christian finds an even stronger and more explicitly soteriological warrant for good works: What we do for the neighbor, we do for *God.* The parable of the Last Judgment (Matt. 25:31-46), like that of the Good Samaritan, is deeply disturbing in its impact.

The experience of judgment is shown here as a moment of revelation. It is the time when the whole Truth is told, when we finally see what meaning our words, our actions, our lives have had. Those who have been obedient to the command to love the neighbor are justified in the sight of God. Although they did not know what they were doing, their obedience has ensured the salvific nature of their actions: "In so far as you did this to one of the least of these . . . , you did it to me" (v. 40). Likewise, those who have neglected the needs of the neighbor, and who also did not know what they were doing, are condemned. In failing to love what God loves, they have failed God Incarnate: "In so far as you neglected to do this to one of the least of these, you neglected to do it to me" (v. 45). If we do not love what God loves, then we have not begun to understand either what God or what love means, and our relationship with our Maker remains one of self-enhancing infatuation.

It is the clear connection between love for the neighbor and God's saving act of love for us—evident in the teachings of both the Old and New Testaments— that distinguishes the biblical command from the natural humanitarian impulse to alleviate suffering. Our own salvation depends on the salvation of the rest of creation, and nothing we can say or do will ever make it otherwise; yet this vital connection between love and salvation is easily obscured.

The Protestant Reformers were correct in insisting that our good works do not win us God's love. But it is the nature of fallen humanity to believe otherwise. If good works can bring about our salvation, then control of the process rests with us; the issues of salvation are in *our* hands. Yet God cannot possibly love us more in the future than he loves us already, and the love with which we love the neighbor is ultimately a "borrowed" love. It belongs to the God who first loved us, and it becomes active in us only at the moment of conversion—what Wesley called "the new birth."

Fear of this pervasive human impulse to control salvation has led to an equally pervasive fear of "works righteousness." The unhappy consequence of this fear seems to be a general severing of the vital biblical connection between love of neighbor and salvation: Good works cannot save us; therefore, good works and salvation are not causally linked. Nevertheless, good works are important, and it is *we* who must perform them. Thus the self that has not yet been enlarged by love for God experiences the command to love the neighbor as a frustrating obligation, an obligation that gives rise to guilt rather than gratitude.

What happens when the soteriological basis for good works evaporates? Do good works cease? No. What happens in the absence of clear theological grounding is reversion either to the natural humanitarian impulse— not bad in itself but in relation to Christian practice, something that falls woefully short of the mark—or to a political program as the basis for the "good society." And each of these solutions to the problem of how to love one's neighbor as oneself is flawed, just as fallen human nature is flawed.

The humanitarian impulse operates on the assumption that all suffering is evil and must be eliminated, or at least mitigated, insofar as this is humanly possible. Because it relies, as it must, on its larger cultural surroundings for its standard of judgment on what constitutes an acceptable "quality of life" and an unacceptable level of suffering, a great leap of the imagination is not required to see how dangerous such a "love" for the neighbor can be. Standards for quality of life vary significantly from one culture to another, even from one individual to another, with prosperous, highly developed societies setting a much higher standard for a minimum quality of life and acceptable level of suffering than would be set by a poor, less developed society. "Love" in one instance—where old age is a burdensome liability—might encourage legalized euthanasia. In another part of the world, where the elderly are venerated, such a response would be unthinkable, despite the presence of senility or debilitating physical conditions.

Here especially, the absence of a soteriological motive is morally dangerous. The biblical witness, contrary to the natural humanitarian impulse, posits a redemptive meaning to some forms of suffering. For Israel and the church, suffering is not always meaningless, nor is it always an evil to be eliminated at all costs. It must be remembered that, in the oddest cosmic choice of all, God *elected* to suffer, by means of cruel injustice, *for us:* "And through his wounds we are healed" (Isa. 53:5). Who would have guessed? Who among us would even have thought of, much less selected, such a strange and unappealing method of deliverance! Yet who among us can presume to say the choice was a bad one? Who among us has not, at some point in life, benefited greatly (at least in a spiritual sense) from some dreadful, unsought suffering, physical or mental, which we nevertheless subconsciously consented to experience?

Christians are called on to alleviate whatever suffering they can without usurping the prerogatives of God, but in so doing they must not succumb to the misconception that equates salvation with the elimination of all suffering. There are situations of intractable, utterly mysterious suffering in which God is at work in ways that are completely hidden from us, and the only appropriate response on our part is repentance.

The second common human response to the neighbor's need is a political program of ideology. Marxism has been the grand secular soteriology of the twentieth century. It is the political program par excellence to eliminate economic inequities and social injustices. Most Westerners are satisfied with less grandiose schemes that do not require so much self-sacrifice, but most social reformers are, like Marx, concerned with bringing about structural changes that are meant to eliminate once and for all the systemic causes of poverty and injustice. Their efforts are directed toward ensuring that vulnerable individuals will no longer be at the mercy of the whims of powerful individuals, and surely this is a worthy goal.

But when in the church the political program or ideology is allowed to operate soteriologically, a strange and mischievous thing happens: A new legalism is born. Proponents of systemic change—which may in certain cases be amply justified—become harshly critical of fellow

Christians whose efforts to love the neighbor are expressed in individual acts of charity. The moralism of the left, like that of the right, demands absolute loyalty to the program: You are either with us or against us. The results of such intemperate zeal can sometimes be ludicrous, as when Christian activists severely criticize Mother Teresa of Calcutta because her work indirectly supports the "system" or because her conservative theology sets her at odds with popular methods of population control. Equally disturbing are the sometimes coercive measures some seminaries have adopted in relation to inclusive language policies. A colleague of mine recently reported hearing a conversation in which a professor at a very prestigious institution announced with great satisfaction that any person in the school using "sexist" language would be shouted down and "not allowed to speak." Where theology languishes, moral elitism flourishes.

The command to love the neighbor must be understood in relation to salvation precisely because it is inescapably linked to the command to love God. Scripture emphatically qualifies love of God by love of neighbor.

> Anyone who says, "I love God,"
> and hates his brother [or sister],
> is a liar,
> since [anyone] who does not love the brother that he can see
> cannot love God, whom he has never seen.
> So this is the commandment that he has given us,
> that anyone who loves God must also love his brother.
>   (I John 4:20-21)

At the same time, it is not possible to fulfill the second command in isolation from the first. We do not love successfully, or obediently, when we try to love out of our own resources. I have often heard people say, "I find God in my neighbor." This of course may be true, provided that the obverse obtains: "I find my neighbor in God." But often this is not the case. The neighbor and the neighbor's welfare become the source of meaning and self-justification for the individual who will not come to terms with the Transcendent—who will not pray. Yet it is in prayer that we discover our neighbor's real worth, as well as our own. Our capacity to love is always born of the discovery that we have been loved "beforehand" (I John 4:19). And that love has to be learned firsthand in the experience of a relationship.

This reality—our need to be loved beforehand— keeps us in a perpetual state of neediness toward God. There is simply no way we can be obedient to the command to love without grafting ourselves onto the vine of Christ: "Whoever remains in me, with me in him, / bears fruit in plenty; / for cut off from me you can do nothing" (John 15:5). The choice set before us is therefore the choice of enlargement or withering. We must either bear fruit through obedience or face a fierce and final pruning.

~ ~ ~

O Lord, who though thou wast rich yet for our sakes didst become poor, and hast promised in thy holy gospel that whatsoever is done to the least of thy brethren thou wilt receive as done to thee: Give us grace, we humbly beseech thee, to be ever willing and ready to minister, as thou enablest us, to the needs of others, and to extend

the blessings of thy kingdom over all the world; to thy
praise and glory, who art God over all, blessed for ever.
                                           —Augustine of Hippo[1]

O Lord, remember not only the men and women of
good will, but also those of ill will. But do not remember
all the suffering they have inflicted on us; remember the
fruits we have bought, thanks to this suffering—our
comradeship, our loyalty, our humility, our courage,
our generosity, the greatness of heart which has grown
out of all this, and when they come to judgement let all
the fruits which we have borne be their forgiveness.

—Prayer written by an unknown prisoner in Ravens-
bruck concentration camp and left beside the body of a
dead child.[2]

DISCUSSION QUESTIONS

1. For clergy: What has been the effect on your own
preaching, teaching, and spiritual practice of a "psychol-
ogized" reading of Leviticus 19:18? Does examining the
text in its larger literary context—while omitting the
affective connotation—pose any new challenges for you?
2. For laity: To what extent have you received the
command to love the neighbor as a burdensome,
guilt-inducing obligation? Would it make a difference if
you began to see service to the neighbor as a kind of
"borrowed" love rooted in Christ's love for you?
3. How would you describe your actual or "operating"
soteriology (doctrine of salvation) in relation to good
works? Are the helpful things you do for the neighbor
done (consciously) *for* God? Are they done to *please*
God? Or is your primary motive the alleviation of
suffering?

4. What have been the spiritual consequences of the tendency to assign "saving" significance to political programs and ideologies that are currently popular in the church?

5. Can you point to any instances of a transformed relationship with the neighbor that has come about as a consequence of the deepening of your own prayer life? What kind of changes had to occur in you before the healing in the relationship could take place?

NOTES

1. *The New Book of Christian Prayers,* ed. Tony Castle (New York: Crossroad, 1986), p. 265.
2. *The Oxford Book of Prayer,* ed. George Appleton (Oxford: Oxford University Press, 1985), p. 112.

— 4 —

The Love of God
and the Sense of Sin

*I am the Lord your God, who brought you out
of the land of Egypt, out of the house of
bondage. You shall have no other gods before
me.* (Exod. 20:2-3 RSV)

Unconditional love is something greatly to be
desired, but it is a scarce good in human relationships.
For the most part, it is not to be found in the marriage
relationship. If it were, the divorce rate would be far
lower than it is. Today's marriage contracts are vivid
testimony to just how conditional the love between the
sexes can be. Mother love is probably the closest thing
we find in human existence to a genuinely unconditional
love, and this is not because women are superior human
beings but because of something that has been tagged
"maternal instinct"—we mothers have been given a
certain biological assist. Even here, we know that many
women fall woefully short of the ideal of a good mother.

But "good" or not, mothers are enormously powerful
people whose love and approval we constantly seek. I
was amused, and very touched, while watching the
Super Bowl in January 1988. Each time the television
camera focused a close-up shot on a victorious athlete,
these enormous, hulking gladiators would mouth the

75

words "Hi, Mom!" Mothers may love us even when we
fail—perhaps especially when we fail—but when we
succeed, we want to be sure they know about it! Their
love for us, their hopes, their dreams and expectations
form the bedrock of the individual psyche, as most
psychotherapists will attest. Our relationships with both
parents are the first, and most formative, relationships of
our entire lives. These two persons are the mirror into
which we look, and the image reflected back to us is
what we believe we are. If Mom loves us and believes in
us, then we are worth loving. If Dad is proud of us and
spends time with us, then we are worthy of respect.

Later in life we look to our friends to act as a mirror for us.
Children and teenagers especially can be ruthlessly cruel
and demanding of one another and of themselves. When
the young person looks into the mirror provided by the
peer group, if she does not see a "perfect" image—that is,
one that looks just like the most popular girl in school: slim,
pretty, and not too bright—she often begins a relentless
campaign of self-improvement. Failure to meet exacting
communal standards usually brings self-deprecation and
despair. The same holds true for young men. There is a set,
very narrow image of appropriately "masculine" behavior.
Usually, it is overtly macho: extremely physical, anti-intel-
lectual, and tinged with a studied insensitivity and cynicism
that goes by the label "cool."

If and when we finally fall in love and that love is
reciprocated, what we see in the mirror of that
relationship is positively redemptive. The love of
another person—especially a person who is strong,
attractive, and worthy of respect—is like a light, a glow
in which we are bathed. Our initial response to this
experience is one of disbelief. It is not possible that such
a one could love *me;* I am not worthy of this affection.

Once he or she finds out what I'm really like, the relationship will disintegrate. The lover has been taken in, and only we know the truth about ourselves.

Eventually, if there is sufficient maturity, patience, and trust, the relationship will survive this mutual disbelief. Time and the knowing that comes from sharing many different types of experiences together convince us that our personal failings are not going to be lethal to the relationship. The love that is shared becomes a shared existence, a union, so that the qualities of character we so admire in the other become a part of us as well. We become what we love. We become what we see reflected back in the mirror the relationship provides.

When the Hebrews exited Egypt, they were a mixed multitude, a spiritually numb and nameless band of frightened and disspirited slaves. But their miraculous deliverance at the Sea forced a radical self-evaluation. They, who were nobody, "no people," were now *somebody:* "God's people." The Love that had brought the entire world into existence had deigned to notice them, had cared enough to intervene in their history. The outstretched arm of Yahweh had actually delivered them from the mighty hand of Pharaoh. What could this mean?

It meant that Pharaoh's Hebrew slaves were worth a great deal more than they had ever dared dream. They who had had to wash the feet of their oppressors had been delivered from destruction by a power mightier than Pharaoh. The love that was now being offered them was a transforming love. The image reflected back to them in the mirror of that divine-human relationship was the image of a free people, chosen by God for a special purpose. What that purpose might be was not yet clear, but that there was a purpose was certain. For Israel knew—just as you and I know—that she did not deserve to be loved like this. She had done nothing to merit it.

If the relationship between Yahweh and Israel begins with an act of unmerited grace on Yahweh's part, it can only continue if Israel responds appropriately to this initiative. Like any relationship, this one required a set of terms, of mutual expectations that spell out what loyalty and fidelity mean in this particular kind of love. If Israel was to be God's free people, she must begin to see herself differently and then live in the light of this new vision.

The terms of this unique relationship were given to Moses on Mount Sinai, where he had first made the acquaintance of the Great I Am. The Decalogue, the Ten Words, is the basis for Yahweh's covenantal relationship with Israel. It is the marriage contract, so to speak, and it begins by affirming Yahweh's exclusive claim to Israel's affection: "You shall have no other Gods except me." The first four commandments, set in the context of worship, deal directly with the issue of loyalty to Yahweh. They spell out what it means to love God with all our heart, soul, strength, and mind. The last six make clear that love of God implies a particular stance toward the neighbor. Yahweh has not become espoused to an individual in this case but to a community—an entire people.

This means that just as there is a collective identity here (God's people), so there must be a loyalty to the collective. To violate the trust or the rights of those Yahweh loves is to offend the One who loves them. If we love God, we must love what God loves. We must treat our neighbor with at least as much honor and respect as we treat ourselves, or as we would wish to be treated by others.

The marriage contract analogy is actually a very ancient one. Scripture, especially the prophets, frequently compares the relationship of Yahweh to the chosen people to that of a marriage. Like many marriages, it is a stormy one. Given the circumstances of the relationship, this is not surprising. The prophet Hosea, who makes his life a parable of this divine-human relationship, willingly chooses a most unsuitable mate: Gomer, a prostitute. Vulnerable and fickle, Gomer perpetually violates the exclusive marriage vow and bears three children, all apparently the result of sinful unions: The first son Hosea names Jezreel (a name that means warfare and bloodshed), the second child (a daughter) is called Unloved, and the third child (another son) becomes No-People-of-Mine. Israel is like Gomer. Her repeated infidelities cause Yahweh endless anguish. Tormented by his bride's ingratitude and rejection, Yahweh promises to frustrate Israel at every turn.

> That is why I am going to block her way with thorns,
> and wall her in so that she cannot find her way;
> she will chase after her lovers and never catch up with them,
> she will search for them and never find them.
> Then she will say, "I will go back to my first husband,
> I was happier then than I am today." (Hos. 2:8, 6, 9, 7)

The consequences of violating the terms of the relationship are described with exquisite accuracy here. Sin—the name we give those violations—appears first in our lives as an offer of something better, something more satisfying and fulfilling than what we already have. When Gomer leaves Hosea she says to herself, "I am going to court my lovers . . . / who give me my bread and water, / my wool, my flax, my oil and my drink" (2:5). But these offers of favors are spurious, and Gomer's assent to them is based on a kind of willful self-deception: "She would not acknowledge, not she, / that *I* was the one who was giving her / the corn, the wine, the oil, / and who freely gave her that silver and gold / of which they have made Baals" (2:8, emphasis mine).

Initially, Yahweh's solution is simply to permit Israel to suffer the consequences of her faithless choice. Spurned, Yahweh returns to his dwelling place: "Until they confess their guilt and seek my face; / they will search for me in their misery" (5:15; 6:1). When the divine support system (grace) is withdrawn—when Yahweh takes back the wool and the flax intended to cover her nakedness—Gomer is left naked and ashamed before the eyes of those elusive lovers whose favors lured her from her rightful husband. When we choose sin, we get what we ask for.

God's strategy—that of leaving us to our own devices when we choose not to obey, not to love—does not suggest a lack of love on Yahweh's part. Nor is it a sign that God's love is conditional after all. I remember as a young adult with strong Calvinist proclivities asking the first Catholic priest I'd ever met why God had permitted even the possibility of sin in the first place. His answer startled me with its simplicity and truthfulness. He said, "If you really love someone, would you want to *force* them to love you? Wouldn't you rather have them choose to love you because they wanted to?" I knew instantly that he was right, and it was only at that

moment that the possibility began to dawn on me of
there being a painful risk for God in the act of creation.

In Israel's case, as in Gomer's, Yahweh trusts that
once the consequences of sin are fully savored, the
original love relationship will begin to look much more
attractive: "That is why I am going to lure her [back],"
says Yahweh,

> and lead her out into the wilderness
> and speak to her heart.
> I am going to give her back her vineyards,
> and make the Valley of Achor
>   [Megiddo or Armageddon] a gateway of hope.
> There she will respond to me as she did when she was
>   young,
> as she did when she came out of the land of Egypt.
>   (2:14-15)

Although Yahweh would be justified in leaving Israel
to her own ruin, it would run counter to the divine
nature to do so. Listen to the words of the prophet
Hosea. Here Yahweh loves with the tender, unconditional love of a mother:

> When Israel was a child I loved him,
> and I called my son out of Egypt.
> But the more I called to them, the further they went
>   from me;
> they have offered sacrifice to the Baals
> and set their offerings smoking before the idols.
> I myself taught Ephraim to walk,
> I took them in my arms;
> yet they have not understood that I was the one looking
>   after them.
> I led them with reins of kindness,
> with leading-strings of love.

I was like someone who lifts an infant close against his
    cheek;
stooping down to him I gave him his food.   (11:1-4)

Even in the face of repeated faithlessness, Yahweh
cannot abandon his chosen ones:

Israel, how could I give you up?
How could I treat you like Admah,
or deal with you like Zeboiim?
My heart recoils from it,
my whole being trembles at the thought.
I will not give rein to my fierce anger,
I will not destroy Ephraim again,
for I am God, not man:
I am the Holy One in your midst
and have no wish to destroy.   (11:8-9)

Faithless Israel is promised—at the very moment of
judgment—reconciliation with her beloved and long-
suffering spouse.

When that day comes—it is Yahweh who speaks—
she will call me, "My husband,"
no longer will she call me, "My Baal [master]."(2:18)

Even her illegitimate children will be owned by God.
Says Yahweh, "I will love Unloved; / I will say to
No-People-of-Mine, 'You are my people,' / and he will
answer, 'You are my God'" (2:23).

The perversity of fallen human nature is such that it
really does not want to be the recipient of unmerited
grace, or the unconditional, "maternal" love of God. We
prefer to earn God's love; we would rather not be
helpless. We would like to be "good." This is why the

Pharisees found it so difficult to accept God's aggressive pursuit of the sinner in the Incarnation. In Jesus we see the unconditional mother love of God determined against all odds to bring the sinner back into fellowship with Yahweh and the chosen people. In Jesus, God takes the initiative to repair the breach, even breaking some rules in so doing!

Why, then, are we so anxious to receive unconditional love from our parents, our friends, and our spouse, and yet find this kind of love so difficult to receive when it comes from God? What precisely is going on here?

Remember that when we seek unconditional love from our human relationships, we are seeking approval and affirmation. We want to believe that we are worthy, lovable, and good; what is more, we want to believe that we are deserving of the love of others. When we look anxiously in the mirror provided by each one of these important relationships what we want most of all is to meet with our *own* approval.

But what happens when we look in the mirror provided by the divine-human relationship? We see what Peter saw: "Leave me, Lord; I am a sinful man!" (Luke 5:8); We see what Isaiah saw: "Woe is me! For I am lost; for I am a man of unclean lips, and I dwell in the midst of a people of unclean lips!" (Isa. 6:5 RSV); or we see Gomer, naked and ashamed, the beloved spouse—rescued from prostitution—yet still feckless, thankless, perpetually self-indulgent.

It is not hard to find Christians who would like to get closer to God, who want a deeper, more satisfying prayer life. They are legion. But the hard, unpalatable fact of the matter is that when we begin to approach God—or allow God to approach us—the first thing we see, the first thing we have to deal with, is our own sinfulness. In the experience of the love of God, we begin to see *in the light of Truth* and those same demons who recognized Jesus for who he was are rudely awakened in us. In order to find God in prayer, we must repent and return in faithful obedience to the terms of the marriage contract.

No serious progress can be made in the spiritual life until we are willing to open our eyes and look at ourselves with ruthless honesty. Sometimes we are given, as a great grace, a sudden sharp vision of our own pettiness, or we may more gradually find ourselves appalled at the depths of hatred, rage, or addiction within us; but such insights are rare. All the classic spiritual traditions, including that of the Wesleys, take this all-too-human resistance to reality into account. The traditional solution to the problem is to structure something into our prayer life which will counteract our natural unwillingness to think about sin.

I speak here of what is commonly known as an "examination" *(examen)* of conscience. It is a reflective exercise in which we review the events of the day, our thoughts, words, and actions all in the light of our relationship to God. This last point is very important. Prayers of gratitude for grace already received, prayers for forgiveness and prayers for grace to avoid sin in the future are all essential to the exercise. In other words, it is not simply a checklist of errors. Generally, it is a conversation, with God, about the state of the relationship. Specifically, it is a careful and very explicit prayer of confession. If you begin to practice the general *examen* of conscience regularly, you will be surprised at the result. It is much more effective than a simple confession of "sin" in general. Why? Because it is like a long, hard look in the mirror that God holds before us, not a passing glance.

The best-known form of the *examen* is that provided in the Spiritual Exercises of St. Ignatius of Loyola. This is not the first instance of the exercise; the actual practice is very ancient. But the model provided by Ignatius has proved to be particularly durable and popular. John Wesley practiced a particularly rigorous *examen*—one much more minutely detailed than the Ignatian version. Listen for a minute to the kind of questioning to which Wesley and other members of the Holy Club submitted themselves as a daily practice:

> Have I been simple and recollected in everything I said or did? Have I (a) been simple in everything, that is, looked upon God, my Good, my Pattern, my one Desire, my Disposer, Parent of Good; acted wholly for him? . . . (b) Recollected? that is, has this simple view been distinct and uninterrupted? . . .
>
> Have I prayed with fervor? at going in and out of church? morning and evening in private? Monday, Wednesday and Friday, with my friends, at rising? before lying down? . . .
>
> Have I duly prayed for the virtue of the day? . . .
>
> Have I duly meditated? . . . What was particular in the Providence of this day? How ought the virtue of the day to have been exerted upon it? How did it fall short? . . .
>
> Have I been zealous to do, and active in doing good? that is, have I embraced every probable opportunity of doing good, and preventing, removing, or lessening evil? . . . Have I thought anything too dear to part with, to serve my neighbor? . . . Have I persuaded all I could to attend public prayers, sermons, and sacraments . . . ?

Have I rejoiced with and for my neighbor in virtue or pleasure? grieved with him in pain, for him in sin? Have I received his infirmities with pity, not anger?[1]

Wesley's *examen* would be daunting, I should think, even to the most scrupulous of today's Christians. A much simpler approach is to take the Ten Commandments—the original "marriage contract"—and use them as a reliable basis for reflecting on the extent to which we have honored God's exclusive claim to our commitment in the daily events of our lives, including and especially those encounters with our neighbor. A structure that is too tightly regimented can lead to tedium and discouragement; insufficient structure takes the "bite" out of the exercise.

Ignatian spirituality currently speaks of an examination of "consciousness" rather than of conscience. Increasingly, the emphasis is being laid not so much on an accounting of actions taken as on the process of discernment. One of the spiritual practices for which Ignatius is most famous is that of the discernment of spirits. Put briefly, discernment entails a very attentive listening to those conflicting voices within us in an effort to discover precisely what God is leading us to. This practice assumes the kind of internal spiritual warfare that Paul speaks of when he says,

> Though the will to do what is good is in me, the performance is not, with the result that instead of doing the good things I want to do, I carry out the sinful things I do not want. When I act against my will, then, it is not my true self doing it, but sin which lives in me.
>
> In fact, this seems to be the rule, that every single time I want to do good it is something evil that comes to hand.   (Rom. 7:18-21)

Understood in this context, the *examen* becomes an opportunity to order our lives in response to what we have discerned. It becomes a method for sensing and recognizing what one writer calls "those interior invitations of the Lord that guide and deepen this ordering from day to day and not [cooperating] with those subtle insinuations opposed to that ordering."[2]

As we begin to get serious about our relationship to God, we become increasingly aware of many particular shortcomings in ourselves. Often we may feel over-whelmed by our limitations. Under these circum-stances, it is important to remember that Christian perfection is the work of a lifetime. As the writer just quoted puts it,

> The Lord does not want all [our defects] to be handled at once. Usually there is one area of our hearts where He is especially calling for conversion which is always the beginning of new life. He is interiorly nudging us in one area and reminding us that if we are really serious about Him this one aspect of ourselves must be changed. This is often precisely the one area we want to forget and (maybe!) work on later. We do not want to let His word condemn us in this one area and so we try to forget it and distract ourselves by working on some other area which *does* require conversion but not with the same urgent sting of consciousness that is true of the former area. It is in this first area of our hearts, if we will be honest and open with the Lord, where we are very personally experiencing the Lord in the burning fire of His Word as He confronts us here and now. So often we fail to recognize this guilt for what it really is or we try to blunt it by working hard on something else that we may want to correct whereas the Lord wants something else here and now.[3]

For this reason, it is helpful to practice what Ignatius referred to as a "particular" *examen* of conscience. Here, we decide to concentrate on a single, frequently recurring sinful disposition or habit. The *examen* begins, upon our rising, with a reminder to ourselves to be especially watchful in relation to this failing throughout the day and includes a brief review of the day after the mid-day meal and again after the evening meal. The Ignatian model of this practice includes keeping a written record of our "slips."

A caveat is in order here. As we have observed, the exercise itself includes prayers of gratitude, petition, and repentance, and it should never be conducted without these. Beyond that, however, the regular practice of the *examen* assumes a steady commitment to prayer, especially contemplative prayer, as the larger life framework. The quality of the *examen* will reflect the quality of our overall prayer life, and its effectiveness will advance in proportion to our efforts to be receptive to God in every facet of our lives.

The beginning of a new discipline is never easy. At first we are apt to feel it stilted or artificial. But the same may be said for prayer itself. I myself spent many years reading books *about* prayer before I actually dared address God personally as a "Thou." And at first it seemed stilted and artificial. But this particular practice will repay our persistent, if awkward, efforts. Perhaps more than any other prayer discipline, the *examen* ensures accountability in the divine-human relationship.

Far from leaving us to our own devices, the unconditional mother love of God calls *us* out of Egypt, lures *us* out of the wilderness, and speaks to *our* hearts. The judgment that we pass on ourselves as we gaze into

the mirror of the divine-human relationship—the vision
of our own unworthiness, our weakness, our absolute
dependence on grace—is the necessary means whereby
we can respond to this invitation. But the initiative
always belongs to God, who promises to turn the valley
of our judgment into a "gateway of hope."

~ ~ ~

Penetrate these murky corners where we hide mem-
ories and tendencies on which we do not care to look,
but which we will not yield freely up to you, that you
may purify and transmute them. The persistent buried
grudge, the half-acknowledged enmity which is still
smouldering; the bitterness of that loss we have not
turned into sacrifice, the private comfort we cling to, the
secret fear of failure which saps our initiative and is
really inverted pride; the pessimism which is an insult to
your joy. Lord, we bring all these to you, and we review
them with shame and penitence in your steadfast light.
                                        —Evelyn Underhill[4]

Forgive them all, O Lord:
our sins of omission and our sins of commission;
the sins of our youth and the sins of our riper years;
the sins of our souls and the sins of our bodies;
our secret and our more open sins;
our sins of ignorance and surprise,
and our more deliberate and presumptuous sin;
the sins we have done to please ourselves
and the sins we have done to please others;
the sins we know and remember,
and the sins we have forgotten;
the sins we have striven to hide from others
and the sins by which we have made others offend;
forgive them, O Lord, forgive them all for his sake,

who died for our sins and rose for our justification,
and now stands at thy right hand to make intercession
   for us,
Jesus Christ our Lord.

                         —John Wesley[5]

DISCUSSION QUESTIONS

1. Is it the case that we seek and prefer unconditional love from other persons more than we do from God? If so, why?

2. Do you agree that no serious progress can be made in the spiritual life until we confront our own sinfulness in a very specific and regular way? To what extent is confession a prominent part of your prayer life?

3. Do you find yourself resisting the kind of full self-knowledge that serious prayer requires? What is the root of that resistance?

NOTES

1. *John and Charles Wesley,* ed. Frank Whaling, The Classics of Western Spirituality Series (New York: Paulist Press, 1981), pp. 85-87.
2. George A. Aschenbrenner, S. J., "Consciousness Examen," in David L. Fleming, S.J., *Best of the Review: Notes on the Spiritual Exercises of Saint Ignatius of Loyola* (St. Louis: Review for Religious, 1983), p. 177.
3. Ibid., p. 181.
4. From *The New Book of Christian Prayers,* ed. Tony Castle (New York: Crossroad, 1986), pp. 78-79. Copyright © 1986 by Tony Castle. Reprinted by permission of The Crossroad Publishing Company.
5. Ibid., p. 79.

The Love of God
and the Crucifixion of Self

*If anyone wants to be a follower of mine, let
him renounce himself and take up his cross
and follow me. For anyone who wants to save
his life will lose it; but anyone who loses his
life for my sake will find it.*

(Matt. 16:24-25)

The cultural ethos that invites us to "be all that we
can be" encourages us to believe that we are, or should
be, in charge of the course our future is taking. We are
free, if we will only claim that freedom, to make the kind
of life choices that will enable us to "feel good about
ourselves." Psychotherapeutic techniques are designed
to enhance self-confidence, self-esteem, self-direction.
Many of us think of ourselves, especially our bodies, as
something to work with, work on, to shape as we see fit.
(Who can fail to notice the blitz of books, magazines,
television programs and, now, videos aggressively
marketing the idea that with sufficient effort we too can
have a flat stomach and firm thighs!) The goal of personal
authenticity suggests that since this is *our* life, we must
claim the right to select the desirable image and direct
the shaping. I remember, too, that as a young wife
anticipating parenthood, I believed I had both the right

and the power to shape the lives of my children as I saw fit. I thought of them as malleable—like clay.

Now, shaping or molding unformed material according to a particular design is complex and requires considerable skill. Picture a lump of clay on a potter's wheel. What will eventually become a useful and perhaps beautiful object begins as a shapeless mass of wet clay, which must be pounded and kneaded until it is of the appropriate consistency. When the material is deemed workable, it is placed on a constantly spinning wheel. The major contours of the pot being formed, or thrown, are shaped as the result of a strong, steady pressure brought to bear in the course of hundreds, perhaps thousands, of revolutions of the wheel.

The potter has to be constantly alert to the precise positioning of the clay, for if the lump of clay is allowed to move off center, the shape is distorted and quickly takes on an asymmetrical appearance. As the work proceeds, the finer details are added, and these final refinements require even more precise and subtle handling. Success depends on good raw material, accurate vision, and a practiced hand. Again and again, the potter must return to the original design.

If you have ever tried to throw a pot on a wheel, you will know what I mean when I say it can be devilishly difficult—almost as difficult as raising children. Needless to say, I learned very quickly—but perhaps not quickly enough—that my children were not going to be so malleable as I had anticipated. And perhaps it is just as well, since my parenting skills left much to be desired. There has been something or Someone else besides my husband and me active in their formation— Someone whose agenda I do not know and cannot hope to control. The lesson that my children do not belong to

me has been a difficult one; it has made me feel like a
slow learner. There is something in me that wants very
much to control the process of their maturing—for their
own good, of course—and each reminder to the contrary
is a kind of rebuke, a little death.

When we consider that in the Christian life *we* are the
lump of clay to be worked on, then the skill of the potter
becomes a matter of critical urgency. Though there is
that in me which would love to be doing the shaping,
that wants the finished product to be absolutely unique
and one-of-a-kind and, yes, "perfect," I am increasingly
disenchanted with this scenario. I, for one, do not want
to trust this shaping to an amateur, which is precisely
what I am. I would like to think that the potter to which
this lump of clay has been entrusted has a keen eye, a
steady hand, and a superb model or prototype from
which to work.

Think, for a minute, about being that lump of clay and
what the shaping might actually feel like. First you must
be worked on between the two hands of the potter. You
must be "softened" by constant and repeated pounding,
kneading, and moistening, for until you have reached
the appropriate consistency, you are quite useless for
the potter's purposes. But once that happens, you are
set in motion. Things happen—fast.

The revolutions of the wheel are what make the
shaping possible, and accompanying each revolution is a
firm, steady pressure that remains absolutely still;
remember, it is the clay that is in motion, not the
potter's hand. That quiet but relentless pressure slowly
but surely begins to alter the shape of the clay: you. As
one new curve or indentation is completed—perfected—the pressure point moves to another remaining,
formless area. The hands of the potter center and

support the pot from within and without as the wheel ceaselessly turns. If the clay remains centered, your final shape will be true. The result will be a fitly turned vessel, ready for firing so that the shape will be permanent and the vessel itself functional. But if the clay is allowed to move off center, the result will be skewed. When that happens the potter pounds the wet clay back into a formless lump and starts all over again.

This analogy is helpful, I think, for understanding how scripture and tradition both present the concept of Christian perfection. The early Church very quickly began to articulate the quest for God in terms of Jesus' command to "be perfect just as your heavenly Father is perfect." It saw that quest in terms of being "shaped"— as a matter of surrendering individual lives to the hand of the Master Potter, who worked from the blueprint of all Creation: the divine Logos or Word of God enfleshed in Jesus of Nazareth.

Contrary to what the world says about the desirability of taking charge of our lives, scripture affirms that we are not the ones to decide what shape we will take: "What right have you, a human being," says Paul,

> to cross-examine God? The pot has no right to say to the potter: Why did you make me this shape? Surely a potter can do what he likes with the clay? It is surely for him to decide whether he will use a particular lump of clay to make a special pot or an ordinary one?
> (Rom. 9:20-21)

Both the result and the course of the shaping are beyond our control. They are the responsibility of the Holy Spirit. If in the long run we find this consoling, in the short run we are likely to find it disconcerting.

Whatever suggests loss of control is almost always threatening. Most of us would rather say yes to God after we have had a chance to examine the blueprint or review the agenda.

This leaves us with an unsettling question: If spiritual formation is actually the work of the Spirit, then what do we think we are doing when we talk about the need for spiritual formation in the life of the individual or in relation to the congregation? Does it even make sense to speak of having a "program" of spiritual formation if in fact the work of formation is *God's* work?

We saw earlier that what we normally call prayer is really a kind of preparation for, or an invitation we issue to, the Holy Spirit to come and pray in us. And although we can never predict or program when the Spirit will pray in us, there are things we can do to increase the likelihood that this will happen. We can make ourselves receptive to the Spirit by placing ourselves in the presence of God, by making time and space in our lives for the Love that made us.

Precisely the same thing applies, I believe, in the matter of spiritual formation. Let us return for a minute to the analogy of the clay being worked by the potter. Although it is true that we do not decide what shape we shall take, our involvement does help to determine how relatively difficult or effortless the shaping will be. This is because human cooperation with divine grace is an issue of "malleability." A fitly turned pot begins as a lump of clay that is soft, yet resilient and free of impurities. Similarly, there are various disciplines we can undertake, or exercises we can perform, that permit our formation with less resistance. And the less resistant we are, the less painful and protracted the initial processing of the raw material will be.

The church has always understood this preparation for
the Spirit's shaping as an essential dimension of
discipleship. Paul (again) expresses this active participa-
tion in our own formation in terms of training for an
athletic competition.

> All the runners at the stadium are trying to win, but only
> one of them gets the prize. You must run in the same
> way, meaning to win. All the fighters at the games go
> into strict training; they do this just to win a wreath that
> will wither away, but we do it for a wreath that will never
> wither. That is how I run, intent on winning; that is how
> I fight, not beating the air. I treat my body hard and
> make it obey me, for, having been an announcer myself,
> I should not want to be disqualified. (I Cor. 9:24-27)

The comparison of the disciple with an athlete in
training is an apt one. The strenuous training the athlete
undergoes is never for its own sake. The relentless,
grinding physical effort, the tedium, the false starts, and
the occasional breakthroughs are all for the sake of
something else. It is the prize for which one trains that
lends value and meaning to the genuine acts of
self-denial that go into the making of an Olympic medal
winner.

The point of any disciplined form of training—the
prize for which one runs—is the freedom that comes
with mastery. The hours the artist spends painstakingly
sketching anatomically correct figures or painting in the
style of the great masters is not for the purpose of
creating another Rembrandt. It is to ensure that the
aspiring artist will master the medium to such an extent
that she will not *have* to paint like Rembrandt. Rather,
the excellence acquired through hours of practice will

permit the creation of new forms whose integrity of expression will speak for itself.

The training in discipleship that is analogous to that of the athlete or artist is commonly referred to as "asceticism." From the Greek *askesis*, asceticism means exercise or practice. Typically the term is used in references to bodily restraint, but it may refer to other forms of self-restraint as well. For the Christian, asceticism is a form of cooperation with divine grace. It is the effort we expend to present the Potter with a more malleable piece of clay. The term "discipline" always connotes the submission of the student or disciple to a master teacher or trainer. It also suggests repeated practice and restraint.

The traditional and systematic practice of various spiritual disciplines assumes that sin is aggressive, stubborn, self-serving, and deceptive. It is not going to disappear without putting up a struggle. So in undertaking a spiritual discipline such as fasting, for instance, we are embarking on a kind of guerrilla warfare, a resistance movement of our own, against all there is within us that wants to resist the pressure of the Master Potter's hand. And that is a choice we are actually free to make. We do not have to engage in this kind of resistance movement, but there can be no deep prayer without the practice of self-denial.

The motive for undertaking a spiritual discipline can never be simply self-improvement—even spiritual self-improvement. As such, it becomes just one more sop we throw to a hungry ego. The free choice to discipline or "mortify" (put to death) self-assertion and self-indulgence must be an act of love, motivated by a desire for union with What we love. Only then is it an appropriate response to what we see in the mirror of the

divine-human relationship. The ultimate discipline—
martyrdom—is the free choice of the person who has
already experienced the death of self in all but the most
final sense of the word. The person who has suffered
countless "little deaths" is the one who is truly
malleable, who will yield most readily to the pressure of
the Potter's hand and come through the firing process
glowing and intact.

Few, if any of us, will be called to martyrdom; but all
of us are called to a series of little deaths in the form of
invitations to restrain or deny self. The first and most
important of these invitations is the call to establish
a relationship with God through consistent, daily
prayer—including weekends! Once you make the
decision to engage in daily prayer, you will almost
certainly meet with a multitude of obstacles: late nights
and consequent oversleeping; house guests who upset
the routine; fatigue; illness, parental responsibilities; or
too many social or professional commitments. Trust me,
there will always be *something* presenting itself as a
legitimate if not insurmountable obstacle as a test to the
strength of your commitment and desire. For the
average Christian, the battle ends right here, even
before it has had a chance to begin. The first little death
comes when we decide that we can in fact do with from
thirty to sixty fewer minutes of sleep than we have
hitherto decided was necessary, and that facing God
before our first cup of coffee and the morning paper is
not a ridiculous thing to do. The next one comes when
we resist the urge, while praying, to check on the
laundry or tend to some other seemingly pressing but
usually innocuous task that has suddenly presented itself
to us as useful or necessary.

For the clergy, a similar little death occurs when they

recognize that their time alone with God—their prayer and spiritual reading—has nothing directly to do with sermon preparation. The first impulse of the seminarian or clergyperson who undertakes this discipline is to start speculating about how this time alone with God will yield some excellent sermon material. Since preaching good sermons is what the clergy are called to do, this possibility is extremely seductive. But the point of the time spent with God is just that: *time spent with God* and not the fulfillment of a professional task. No one will argue that a serious commitment to prayer will not have a beneficial effect on preaching; but because the temptation to insist on a visible and immediate outcome of our efforts is so strong, I always urge my students not to use for devotional scripture study a text they plan to preach from. It is the preacher, not the sermon, who is being worked on in that time alone with God. Authentic prayer begins with the understanding—usually hard won—that we are not supposed to "get" anything out of it. We do not pray in order to feel inspired or better about ourselves. We pray *to establish contact with God.* We pray for the sake of and for the love of God and not for the favors and graces that prayer may, and often does, bring us. The willingness to show up for prayer day after day, even when nothing seems to be happening, is a sign that the discipline is beginning to have the desired effect. We have become a little more pliable, and whether we feel anything or not, we are being worked on.

The prevailing form of asceticism in the Christian life has always been fasting. The scriptures link fasting with preparation for prayer, repentance, and almsgiving; and although Jesus taught his disciples that they need not fast while the bridegroom was with them, he also demonstrated, as in the case of the healing of the epileptic boy, that there were certain types of evil that could only be countered by the kind of spiritual power that comes from combining prayer with fasting (see Matt. 17:21 KJV). His own response to his baptism and anointing with the Holy Spirit was a rigorous and lengthy fast in the wilderness of Judea.

The Jews and early Christians both made use of fasting in relation to the liturgical cycle. For example, the Day of Atonement was a day of ritual mourning and prescribed fasting for Jews. In Judaism, fasts were typically undertaken in times of mourning, of national defeat and humiliation, when facing danger, or for purposes of intercession. In Jesus' time the Pharisees fasted twice a week—an expression of repentance in anticipation of the messianic Kingdom. Likewise, John the Baptist's spartan diet of locusts and wild honey was an expression of repentance and anticipation. Fasting twice weekly, on Wednesdays and Fridays, was accepted practice in the church by the end of the first century, and lengthy, very rigorous fasts soon became the norm for the penitential seasons.

Like any spiritual practice, fasting can become a source of pride—a kind of "work" or method for receiving divine approval. This attitude is fatal to prayer, and fasting is also a kind of prayer: It is a way of praying with our bodies. Recognizing this all too human proclivity to turn religious observation to personal gain, Jesus warned his disciples to fast secretly so that they would not be tempted to elicit the admiration of others.

The response of the Protestant Reformers to the practice of fasting was generally one of suspicion. Fasting was not forbidden but nothing of the sort was to be legislated; it had to be a voluntary decision on the part of the person fasting. As a consequence, the practice of fasting in Protestantism soon all but disappeared; and if you have ever undertaken a voluntary fast, it will not be hard to understand why. Wesley, on the other hand, was enthusiastic about the virtues of fasting. He and other members of the Holy Club fasted faithfully twice a week, and fasting continued to be a popular devotional practice among the early Methodists.

In recent times moderate fasting has once again become a more popular practice, partly because it has been seen to be advantageous for health. Persons who fast report that once they get beyond the unpleasant sensation of hunger pangs, they experience a general mental clarity and sometimes even an increase, rather than a decrease, in energy. A kind of inner physical purgation occurs when we give our digestive system a rest from its usual—probably rather high—level of activity. But undertaking a fast for the physical benefits it brings has nothing to do with praying with the body.

What spiritual benefit, if any, can we expect to receive from fasting? My own experience with fasting, which is relatively recent in my life, is probably fairly typical. What I have discovered is that fasting tells me a great deal about myself in an extremely effective way. What it tells me, first of all, is that I am a severely limited, bodily creature and utterly dependent on something outside myself for my life, namely, *food.*

What can happen to us when our stomachs are empty is amazing. We get irritable and short-tempered; maybe our head begins to ache. We may find it hard to concentrate on the task at hand because we are daydreaming about our next meal. Then we find ourselves snapping at our neighbor and we think, "This is counterproductive. I can be a much better Christian if I don't fast." True? I don't think so.

It is immensely sobering and humbling to come face to face with our own limitations in this way. To see yourself ready to kill for a candy bar is to see yourself in a new and rather devastating light. We are not particularly strong; we are not in control. Without a ham sandwich in sight, we too are suddenly "poor" and dependent. The hunger we feel becomes a great leveler, a pointed reminder that it is only the grace of God that holds us in existence at all. We have no reason to be self-congratulatory. From our new, less exalted perspective, both God and neighbor do not look the way they did before. Suddenly the amount of food we customarily consume looks prodigal, for it is clear we could survive on much less.

Famished and tempted to turn stones into bread, Jesus clung to a scriptural promise and talked back to Satan: Mortals do not live by bread alone, but by every word of God (Luke 4:4). When we go temporarily without that which we depend on to sustain us, we are readying ourselves for a different dependence. The emptiness inside us is a new kind of openness, a place where grace may enter and reside. The hunger we feel for bread "makes present" the deeper hunger we feel for God. To be empty is to be prepared to be filled.

Our efforts at fasting may begin with the choice to skip a single meal, or to cut our portions in half. A weekly day of abstinence from solid food is not unusual or particularly heroic for a serious Christian. Periodic abstinence from particular foods such as meat or from alcohol is another small gift of self—a little death—that we can offer. However strenuous or modest our fasts may be, our common human dependence on food makes fasting a universally effective act of devotion. When practiced in a regular way in response to communal worship, it is a remarkably effective common witness to faith in God and solidarity with the poor.

Difficult as bodily mortification may be, there are other forms of self-denial and self-restraint that are equally challenging because they address less physical and therefore less obvious kinds of self-indulgence which are nonetheless spiritually dangerous. Lack of emotional restraint can cause grief, pain, and destruction in human relationships. An undisciplined imagination may make us ineffectual at work or prayer. An ignorant, untrained intellect results in prejudice and an inordinate or "greedy" curiosity. An unchastened will sees no danger in self-serving choices, in impulsive or unthinking action or in no action at all—the sin of sloth. And what is worse than the undisciplined tongue? In the book of James, we read that the person who can control the tongue can control every other part of the self:

> Once we put a bit into the horse's mouth, to make it do what we want, we have the whole animal under our control. Or think of ships: no matter how big they are, even if a gale is driving them, the man at the helm can steer them anywhere he likes by controlling a tiny rudder. So is the tongue only a tiny part of the body, but it can proudly claim that it does great things. Think how small a flame can set fire to a huge forest; the tongue is a flame like that. Among all the parts of the body, the tongue is a whole wicked world in itself: it infects the whole body; catching fire itself from hell, it sets fire to the whole wheel of creation. Wild animals and birds, reptiles and fish can all be tamed by man, and often are; but nobody can tame the tongue—it is a pest that will not keep still, full of deadly poison.   (James 3:3-8)

The mortification of the tongue is surely the harshest and most difficult discipline of all. No "little" death, it represents a significant—often a sacrificial—surrender of self-interest.

Historically, Christians have been willing at times to say no to something that is perfectly good and lawful in itself but which, in our own life circumstances, represents a particularly compelling invitation to self-indulgence. Consider, for example, the way in which many of us react to depression or disappointment. We decide to "do something for ourselves." We tell ourselves, "You deserve a break today." In my own case, I like to console myself with an injection of chocolate or a trip to the mall. What I'm doing, in either case, is distracting myself from whatever is causing me pain by engaging in what looks like harmless self-indulgence. Just as an aspirin deadens the pain of a headache or masks the symptoms of some other ailment, so these little distractions have a druglike effect in dulling the pain or in turning our attention elsewhere. But we can become more practiced at identifying these impulses and evasions for what they are, and the more often we choose to forgo these so-called innocent pleasures, the freer we will be. The choice to face the pain places us once again in a dependent stance before God—always the most advantageous position when it comes to being a recipient of grace.

The same may be said for the drive we all experience to be physically, mentally, and emotionally comfortable and quickly gratified in all our needs. Consider the typical American reaction—that of fury—to being kept waiting. Long lines and heavy traffic, not to mention the discipline of using public transportation or car pools, offer endless opportunities for self-restraint, for "little deaths" to the impatient, insatiable self.

It should be obvious by now that we don't have to look far for opportunities to practice a modest, prudent asceticism. It is in the daily ordinariness of our family life, our work, and our worship that we find the most—and the most fruitful—invitations to "die daily" (I Cor. 15:31). There is more to all this, of course, than the isolated victory over a momentary opportunity for self-indulgence. Each "no" to self, each little death we endure, contributes to the development of a kind of spiritual resilience which, when we are tempted to do something seriously wrong, makes the temptation that much easier to resist.

It needs to be stated plainly that our efforts to discipline ourselves will not be successful if we rely exclusively on our own resources. Even the desire to submit to a very "little" death is the consequence of the prior operation of grace in our lives, and it is only through a continued appeal to grace that we can hope to survive the pounding, pulling, and pummelling life inflicts, with or without the intentional effort to mortify self.

It also needs to be said that the process of purification must proceed beyond what our own grace-assisted efforts can achieve. The consequences of original sin infect every layer of our being, including those we have no real access to, such as the subconscious levels of the psyche. The sin that festers at the center of our being can only be eradicated in the furnace of God's love—not ours. When the clay has been brought to the right consistency and then patiently centered and lovingly shaped on the relentless wheel of ordinary existence, it is finally ready for the fierce judgment of the kiln where

its ultimate worth will be tested. Yet virtually everything that precedes this moment contributes to the
outcome: the quality of the raw material, its strength and
suppleness, the skill and artistry of the Potter—even the
precise heat of the oven and the length of time spent in
the firing. When all these variables function in harmony,
the final product is a flawless vessel, perfectly empty,
ready to be filled.

~ ~ ~

Have mercy on us, Lord, have mercy on us! You are our
Potter and we are the clay. Somehow or other we have
held together until now; we are still carried by your
mighty hand, and we are still clinging to your three
fingers, faith, hope, and charity, with which you support
the whole great bulk of each—that is to say, the whole
weight of your holy Church. Cleanse our reins and our
hearts by the fire of your Holy Spirit, and establish the
work that you have wrought in us, lest we be loosed
asunder and return again to clay or nothingness. We
were created for you by yourself, and toward you our
face is set. We acknowledge you our Maker and Creator;
we adore your wisdom and pray that it may order all our
life. We adore your goodness and mercy, and beg them
ever to sustain and help us. You who have made us,
bring us to perfection; perfect in us the image and
likeness of yourself for which you made us. Amen.
—William of Saint-Thierry[1]

DISCUSSION QUESTIONS

1. What has been the relationship between love and
self-denial in your life?

2. Can you look back over your life and see the ways in which a series of "little deaths" has freed you to be more faithful in your love of God and neighbor? What were some of these "little deaths"?

3. To what extent have you operated on the assumption that you ought to be "getting something" out of your prayer life? What effect has this assumption had on your actual practice of prayer?

4. What has been your experience with fasting?

NOTE

1. M. Basil Pennington, *Pocket Book of Prayers* (Garden City, N.Y.: Doubleday Image Books, 1986), p. 113.

6

The Love of God
and the Communion of Saints

*As the Father sent me, so am I sending
you.*   (John 20:21)

Do you remember how old you were the last time
someone asked you, "What do you want to be when you
grow up?" When I was a youngster in grammar school
that question was always an important one, as it
continued to be later in high school and college when I
began to think not just about an occupation but of having
some kind of "mission" in life. I couldn't have told you
then why it was so important, but I sensed that it was.
Whatever the answer we gave or received, it revealed
something significant about our interests, values, and
dreams. If you wanted to be friends with someone, you
had to find out what they were going to be.

It's funny, but now that I teach adults ranging in age
from their mid-twenties to retirement age, I find this
question still being asked. Usually, the question is
framed not in terms of a personal destiny in life or
engagement in a transcendent cause but in terms of
finding an appropriate form of ministry. "I don't know
yet," they say, "what my ministry will be." The
assumption is that sooner or later they are going to find
out—by graduation, they hope. The fact that most of

them are in a Master of Divinity program and headed for
ordination doesn't seem entirely to settle the issue for
my students. To be honest, I was the same way when I
entered seminary at the age of thirty-four. Rapidly
approaching middle age, I had no clear sense of where
this journey was going to lead me.

But that was only part of the problem. I think what really
lies behind this question is the feeling most of us have that
we have not yet really "grown up," because we have not yet
achieved the sense of mastery and competence in life that
we as children always assumed an adult must somehow
have. Grown-ups are supposed to be secure in their
identity, unafraid, effective, purposeful. But for the most
part, we are not like that. We keep clinging to the idea that
around the next corner that elusive sense of clarity,
purpose, and direction we crave will be there waiting for us.
Things will suddenly all fall into place.

This is especially true, I think, if what we do for an
occupation is in response to a divine "call." A call is
certainly supposed to settle things. Either God or the
bishop tells us where we belong and that's that! So why
is it that so many of us religious professionals are not sure
that we've really landed—that we've found out what it is
we're going to be, now that we are "grown up"?

Now, a parallel question: What does it mean to be in
ministry, and why do so many people these days want to
claim that word for what they do or hope to do? The
"ministry of the laity" is currently a popular concept in
most denominations. We speak of "lay ministries" or
"lay caregiving." Usually this type of lay ministry is
understood as roles performed in the local church
setting—once thought to be the exclusive purview of the
ordained minister. Increasingly, seminaries are en-
rolling students who do not anticipate being ordained

but who, like myself, envisage themselves working for the church in some other capacity. Almost anything one now does as a church member is likely to be referred to as a ministry.

This rather free use of the term "ministry" and its common connection to specifically ecclesial roles or actions of one sort or another may not be entirely helpful. *Ministry* has become such a popular and, I think, overworked term, I fear it is in danger of becoming quite meaningless. Further, I am uncomfortable when people assume that teaching in seminary constitutes "my ministry" or "my mission" in life. I never speak of it in those terms. For one thing, I keep finding more corners to turn. For another, I think it is theologically incorrect to collapse together the career choice to work full-time for the church with ministry or mission as if they were a single category. I have come to the realization that I may never know—at least this side of the grave—what my mission or purpose in life is in regard to the divine economy. And what is more, this is probably the way it should be.

This is not because I have failed to grow up or make hard choices. Nor is it because I have not yet achieved the mastery or competence that I learned as a child to associate with adulthood—I doubt anyone ever does! It is because I have finally gotten just a glimpse of the mysterious connection between prayer and mission and the way in which both these realities are a consequence of what the church calls the communion of the saints.

The full and loving surrender of the self to God entails first of all the surrender of autonomy as the secular society understands it. Baptism is the sacrament of surrender. In the choice to die and rise with Christ, we consent to hand over that autonomous existence in

exchange for a new status of total dependence and
interdependence. To become part of the Body whose
head is the Lord Jesus is to cast one's lot with perfect,
crucified Love. Even to speak of being a "member" of
this Body does not do real justice to the kind of union
Paul is trying to express with this image. For many, the
word *member* suggests a loose conglomeration of
separate identities. It would be much better, said the
late Bishop John A. T. Robinson, if we described
ourselves as "membranes" of the body:

> It is almost impossible to exaggerate the materialism
> and the crudity of Paul's doctrine of the Church as
> literally now the resurrection *body* of Christ. The
> language of "membership" of a body corporate has
> become so trite that the idea that the individual can be a
> "member" has ceased to be offensive. The force of Paul's
> words can today perhaps be got only by paraphrasing:
> "Ye are the body of Christ and severally membranes
> thereof." (I Cor. 12:27) The body that he has in mind is
> as concrete and as singular as the body of the
> Incarnation. His underlying conception is not of a
> supra-personal collective, but of a specific personal
> organism. He is not saying anything so weak as that the
> Church is a society with a common life and governor,
> but that its unity is that of a single physical entity:
> disunion is dismemberment.[1]

It is in the death and resurrection of Christ—which
baptism permits us to share—that separate selves, even
warring races, become "one" (meaning a *single*) new
entity. This is what Paul means when he speaks of Christ
ending the enmity between Jew and Gentile:

> For he is the peace between us, and has made the two
> into one and broken down the barrier which used to

keep them apart, actually destroying in his own person
the hostility caused by the rules and decrees of the Law.
This was to create *one single New Man* in himself out of
the two of them and by restoring peace through the
cross, to unite them both in a single Body and reconcile
them with God. In his own person he killed the
hostility. Later he came to bring the good news of peace,
peace to you who were far away and peace to those who
were near at hand. Through him, both of us have in the
one Spirit our way to come to the Father.

(Eph. 2:14-18, emphasis mine)

Until relatively recently, I always thought of the "new
creation in Christ" as having been a renewed individual.
This is a typically modern and especially Western bias
that I brought to the passage. The New English Bible
helps to perpetuate this misreading when it speaks of the
creation of one new "humanity" by the act of divine
reconciliation. But such a notion is, I am convinced,
quite foreign to what Paul was talking about. His vision
entails a union much more intimate than anything I ever
dreamed of.

Speaking of this body to the church at Corinth, Paul
clarifies what baptism means for our identity. The body
is not, he claims,

to be identified with any one of its many parts. If the foot
were to say, "I am not a hand and so I do not belong to
the body," would that mean that it stopped being part of
the body? If the ear were to say, "I am not an eye, and so
I do not belong to the body," would that mean that it was
not a part of that body? If your whole body was just one
eye, how would you hear anything? If it was just one ear,
how would you smell anything?   (I Cor. 12:14-17)

This means a great deal more than that we simply "need" one another—that we all have different gifts to share, different strengths and weaknesses—though of course this is true. What it means is that *my* identity depends on *yours*. It means that I cannot fully be what I am called to be—namely, a new creature in Christ— unless you too are transformed. I cannot stand alone as an eye, an ear, a hand, or a foot. I have neither identity nor function apart from the operation of the whole. And whatever affects one part of the Body, for good or for ill, affects me in precisely the same way. Such is the meaning of Christian communion or what tradition calls the communion of saints.

The ethical implications of this vision of the church are profound and very difficult to swallow. Most of us do not really think in these terms. If we did, we could never say things like, "That may be true—or right—for you, but not for me." We could not imagine even the possibility of "doing our own thing." As parts (membranes) of a single organic entity, we cannot act in isolation, even if we wanted to. What is true or good for me must be true and good for my fellow Christian. If it is not, it is *neither true nor good*. The command to love our neighbors as we love ourselves can only be correctly understood in the light of this kind of intimate union in which the future and fate of one is inextricably linked to the future and fate of the other.

As an illustration, consider the by-now commonly accepted phenomenon of divorce as the solution to a troubled marriage. The world around us claims that the decision to divorce must be an individual choice made on the basis of what is best for the individual. Personal happiness and satisfaction are primary goods in American society. (Doesn't the Constitution ensure our right to pursue happiness?) I do not know whether divorce is as frequent within the church as it is without it, but I know it is an increasingly common occurrence; and from what I can see, the basis on which the decision to divorce is most often made by Christians remains the issue of *individual* happiness and well-being. Perhaps it is true that the divorce of a Christian couple does bring a degree of happiness and relief to at least one, if not both, of the persons involved. But what does it do to the community? Does the fracturing of the marriage bring happiness and relief to the Body? Almost never. It brings pain, disappointment, discouragement, and scandal. In this way the fracturing of the family unit becomes a wound inflicted on the larger Body. Yet how many Christians would understand what we were talking about if we were to suggest that perhaps they should reconsider their decision because of the impact it would have on the church? How many would consider valid this claim on their loyalty and commitment?

For the same reason that a Christian cannot legitimately speak of "doing my own thing," it is misleading for the individual Christian to speak of *my* ministry or *my* mission. There can only be one mission in which we as members of the Body are privileged to participate in some very small and partial way. The one mission in which we participate is the mission, the "sending," of God *by God.* God the Father sends God the Son for the healing of the world and God the Spirit in the name of the Son for the sanctification of the world. Healing and holiness are the mission of God. Healing for the sake of holiness and holiness for the sake of consummation—union. Well then, in what sense does God send us? Only in the sense that we are *in Christ*—only so far as we are functioning members (membranes) of that Body in communion with one another are we sent. God does not say, "I give you this particular mission and somebody else a different one." The mission is always the same. The agenda and the task belong to God. We are involved only if we belong to God—if we have said yes to the invitation to sell all that we have and follow Christ.

What practical difference does it make to start thinking in these terms? Suppose we no longer speak of "my" ministry or mission. That doesn't change the reality that we are sent to different places to do different kinds of things: preach, teach, witness in the workplace, evangelize, administer, or heal. That doesn't change the fact that some of us still don't know what we want to do when we grow up!

On the face of it, nothing may change; but in reality, once this surrender of self has occurred—when we do in fact belong to God and live *in Christ*—then everything is as Paul says it will be: new. In the first place, recognizing that the mission is God's and not ours removes an enormous weight from our shoulders. We do not have to decide what our mission will be, when it will be, or how it will be. It simply will be. In the second place, once we begin to understand what it means to be a "membrane" in the Body of Christ, we will worry less about who is being served by means of us. We will begin to see that each small prayer we pray or act we perform is having an effect—usually a hidden one—on the entire Body. We are not free to choose which part of the body our efforts will benefit. All benefit by our faithfulness; all suffer in our defection. By the same token, we will perhaps never know the extent to which our own burdens have been eased by the prayers of the saints—those here below and those in glory.

The fundamental insight here about the essential connection between mission *(missio)* and communion *(communio)* is one that is often ignored or lost sight of: Although it is the sending of God that restores communion, it is communion that allows us to participate in the sending of God. For us, *communion precedes mission*. Our involvement in the sending of God presupposes our union with God and with one another. The union is certainly a union of wills. We must intend what God intends. But if Paul was right, it is more than a union of wills; it is an organic, in some sense, a physical or substantial union as well. Just as husband and wife become "one flesh" in the act of union, so the individual submitting to baptism undergoes a change *in being* and is "substantially" joined to the Body of crucified Love.

If baptism is the sacrament of surrender, then surely eucharist is the sacrament of sending. In consuming the body and blood of our Lord Jesus Christ, we are consummating that substantial union with him. We are becoming one flesh and in that act of uniting, our destiny is sealed. Where he is, we must be; where he goes, we must go. We do not carry him with us. He carries us with him. What he unites himself with becomes a part of us. What he chooses for himself we receive.

The idea of mission is critical to the identity of the "people called Methodist." The ethos of the Wesleyan tradition and certainly of the seminary in which I teach is one in which service to the neighbor is central. The average seminarian and the typical clergyperson I encounter feel at least a smoldering—if not a burning—desire to do more for a hurting world and to be effective in what they do. This is a fundamental value within the tradition, but it does not always uniformly inspire. In

some cases—especially when mission is interpreted
specifically as support for particular causes—it becomes
a source of contention or frustration and burnout.

My conviction is that this contention, frustration, and
burnout are the consequence of the tendency to
separate mission from communion. The most common
expression of this unfortunate separation is the simplistic equating of mission with social action instead of with
the action of grace. If mission is social action, then
mission is something *we* do. National boards and local
church councils make decisions about what "their"
mission will be. Sermons are preached admonishing the
laity to "get involved." Funds are raised, programs are
planned and executed. In some cases, genuine social
improvement results. Most often, the problems do not
go away, despite persistent efforts and sometimes
sacrificial commitments of time and energy.

Another expression of this separation of communion
and mission comes in the very common division made
between prayer and action. How many sermons have I
heard preached to the effect that we can't just "pray"
about something but must take action! Such exhorta-
tions betray a very low view of the efficacy of prayer, an
inability to trust the One to whom prayer is directed.
Prayer is always, if it is anything at all, an affirmation of
trust in the willingness and ability of God to act. When
we separate prayer and action, we are claiming *for
ourselves* the primary power to act, to heal, to reconcile.

If there is only one mission and that mission is the
sending of God by God, then prayer is not something we
do "in addition"; prayer, as the basis for our union with
God, is the *primary* means by which we participate in
the sending of God. This is especially true in the case of
liturgical prayer, where the Body re-presents its unity

and solidarity—especially in the eucharist. But it is true, too, of private and contemplative prayer. There are in the universal church religious communities of contemplative men and women whose lives are devoted exclusively to prayer. Their prayers, which are offered on our behalf, are part of the sending of God by God for the healing of the world.

The separation of mission from communion also tends to focus our attention on the results of our efforts. Action that does not yield visible or measurable results is seen as ineffectual, and this leads to discouragement and burnout. Consider what happened when God sent God for the healing of the world: "He was in the world / that had its being through him, / and the world did not know him. / He came to his own domain / and his own people did not accept him" (John 1:10-11).

On the face of it, the actions of Jesus as a man were ineffectual; his mission failed. The miracle of grace we call the Resurrection was entirely a work of God and none of the events of Jesus' earthly ministry, wonderful as they were, would be remembered today were it not for the Resurrection.

What right do we have, then, to demand an immediate return on our investments of love? How do we know that what appears as a failure in our eyes has contributed nothing to God's purposes? If our mission, our ministry, is the outcome of communion—of prayer—then it is not ours but God's, and we can trust that the divine purposes are being served, even when they remain entirely hidden to us. Might it not be possible that the prayers we pray and the sacrifices we make in our efforts to heal one particular hurt are applied by God to something entirely different? And isn't it possible that God can do something with our personal suffering, our sense of uselessness and ineffectiveness? Are we equally willing to be "laid aside" for God as well as "employed"? Are we ready to be "empty" as well as "full"?

If union with God is the goal of Christian perfection, then the means to that end is the communion of the saints. We cannot by our own power ever love enough or find in our own resources sufficient strength of will to resist the attraction of sin. The elusive vision of competent maturity that kept us pushing forward when we were children is ultimately a cheat. It teases us into believing that the source of that competence and security should reside in us, and that there is something wrong with us if it doesn't. Perfect love is ultimately a communal project, something that we come to together because we are all one Body.

On the night he was betrayed, knowing that when the shepherd was gone the sheep would be scattered, Jesus prayed to the One who had sent him on behalf of his disciples that they might remain in communion with one another:

> Now at last they know
> that all you have given me comes indeed from you;
> for I have given them
> the teaching you gave to me,
> and they have truly accepted this, that I came from you,
> and have believed that it was you who sent me.
> I pray for them;
> I am not praying for the world
> but for those you have given me,
> because they belong to you:
> all I have is yours
> and all you have is mine,
> and in them I am glorified.

I am not in the world any longer,
but they are in the world,
and I am coming to you.
Holy Father,
keep those you have given me true to your name,
so that they may be one like us.

(John 17:7-11)

The bond of their unity, he told them, would be love. His legacy to them, therefore, was a commandment to love. The command to love their neighbor as they loved themselves they knew already. Each one had learned it in the bosom of his family. But this final commandment from their Lord was new: "I give you a new commandment," Jesus said. "Love one another; / just as I have loved you, / you also must love one another" (John 13:34). The new commandment was for those who belong to God the Father to love *as God the Son had loved*. The sending of God by God was the sending of Love—a crucified Love willing to lay down its life for friends and enemies alike. Your mission and mine— which we can only perform insofar as we are in communion with God and with one another—is to submit, out of love for one another, to countless, daily "little deaths" until we have yielded every least and last remnant of self to the purposes of Christ.

~ ~ ~

God has created me to do Him some definite service. He has committed some work to me which He has not committed to another. I have my mission—I may never know it in this life, but I shall be told it in the next. Somehow I am necessary for His purposes, as necessary in my place as an Archangel in his. If, indeed, I fail, He can raise another, as He could make the stones children of Abraham. Yet I have a part in this great work. I am a link in a chain, a bond of connection between persons. He has not created me for nothing. I shall do good, I shall do His work. I shall be an angel of peace, a preacher of truth in my own place, while not intending it, if I do but keep His commandments and serve Him in my calling.

Therefore I will trust Him. Whatever, wherever I am, I can never be thrown away. If I am in sickness, my sickness may serve Him; in perplexity, my perplexity may serve Him. If I am in sorrow, my sorrow may serve Him. My sickness, or perplexity, or sorrow may be necessary causes of some great end, which is quite beyond us. He does nothing in vain. He may prolong my life, He may shorten it. He knows what He is about. He may take away my friends, He may throw me among strangers, He may make me feel desolate, make my spirits sink, hide the future from me—still He knows what He is about.

—John Henry Cardinal Newman[2]

DISCUSSION QUESTIONS

1. What practical differences might it make for us when we think of mission as the sending of God by God?
2. To what extent have you separated mission from communion? What have been the consequences of this separation in your prayer life and practice of ministry?
3. The example of individual happiness as the primary motivating factor in divorce was used to illustrate the radical ethical consequences of Paul's understanding of the communion of saints as members (membranes) of

the Body of Christ. What are the implications of this understanding of Christian communion in relation to other vexing social and personal issues?

NOTES

1. John A. T. Robinson, *The Body* (1952; reprint, Philadelphia: Westminster Press, n.d.), p. 51.
2. *Lead Kindly Light: A Devotional Sampler,* ed. Hal M. Helms (Orleans, Mass.: Paraclete Press, 1987), p. 7.

Going on to Perfection in the Local Congregation

Some Practical Assistance for the Laity

A vast, unfed spiritual hunger is present in the churches today. Increasingly, the laity are asking for much more explicit instruction and support in the spiritual life. Increasingly, they are willing to take the initiative and assume leadership responsibilities in feeding that hunger. It is clear to many Christians that faithful attendance at Sunday worship and active involvement in the programmatic life of the church, important as they may be, are not enough.

One indicator of this growing hunger for a deeper involvement with the Divine is the explosion of new materials (such as this book) being written on the subject of prayer and spirituality. For the most part, this is a healthful development, a cause for rejoicing. When the student is ready, as the saying goes, the teacher appears.

A second indicator has been the response of the churches themselves. Considerably more attention is being given now to issues of spiritual formation both for clergy and laity; retreats of various types and small group structures abound. With typical American "can do" gusto and determination, the churches are out to correct the problem. This, too, is reason for optimism. But caution is in order.

In the first place, the spiritual life is not simply one problem among many to be solved. It is *the* problem of existence, *per se,* and all the books we write and all the programs we implement will not "solve" it for us. The great danger for the American church lies in our perpetual inventiveness, our need to fix what is broken, our obsession with what is new and with technique. These cultural peculiarities predispose us to view the spiritual life as a "problem" in the first place and then create in us the expectation that the problem can be solved with the proper tools and techniques. Hence the spate of books and programs designed to address our spiritual needs. Ironically, as long as we treat these responses as tools and techniques, they will be of very little real assistance. Why?

There is one fundamental insight without which we will remain forever hungry, forever athirst, and that is this: The spiritual life does not consist in a given practice, technique, or program. The spiritual life consists—entirely—in a *relationship.* This relationship has both personal and communal dimensions, neither of which can be neglected. While conservative churches have tended to stress the personal dimension at the expense of the communal, the mainline churches have done just the opposite. What is needed is a personal spirituality that arises from and is directed toward the corporate Body, as well as communal practices and structures that support the individual's personal relationship with God. And it is to this last point—the special weakness of the mainline churches—that I wish to speak.

Cheap, slick, and ever-present talk about what it means to have a "personal savior" has caused many people to shelve the idea altogether. These overly smug, trivializing expressions of Christian piety have little to recommend them and have sometimes caused real spiritual injury. But the fact that this most important of all relationships is so easily misrepresented should not deter us from finding a way of envisioning, articulating, and living out a personal relationship with God that is "saving." Indeed, we must find the means to do so or risk losing the pearl of great price.

The problem is not that we need a whole new way of thinking about this issue. What we need is a longer, more biblically and historically informed perspective; and that, of course, is the point of a little book such as this. We need to stop reacting defensively to a truncated version of the gospel and start to position ourselves to get the whole story. For Christians in the Wesleyan tradition, this means taking a second—or, as the case may be, a first—look at the ways in which Wesleyan spiritual practice provides support for that one all-important relationship.

Perhaps the most significant sign of spiritual renewal in United Methodism today is the systematic attempt on the part of the denomination to reinstitute, in modified form, the original Methodist class meeting. The special usefulness of this particular type of small-group structure for the church today is that it provides what the mainline churches have for the most part failed to supply: a communal structure (not a "program") designed to support the individual's personal relationship with God.

Let us imagine, for the sake of an example, that you have found my arguments convincing, your heart has been touched, or you have felt personally challenged. You would like to establish a loving, intimate relationship with your Maker through your Savior: Jesus Christ. Then what? Must you go it alone, or are there others who would like to share this quest with you? And can all of you, by sharing the joys and struggles attendant upon the journey toward Christian perfection, reach your destination that much faster? If two or three or more of you are willing to gather together regularly to encourage, admonish, and otherwise support one another, isn't it possible that individual lives might be changed in a substantial way? And might it not be the case that through the powerful witness of a few, many other lives might be affected in less direct but nonetheless important ways? What might the impact be on the life of the congregation as first one and then another and another of these small cells of intentional discipleship gradually emerged?

The churches are already accustomed to providing support groups of various sorts, including groups intended for people involved in particular kinds of whole or broken relationships: young parents, the widowed and divorced, and so on. The class meetings (as they were called) or Covenant Discipleship groups (the current designation for a popular modification of the class meeting) operate in precisely the same way. They provide a reliable structure in which people who are seeking help with a particular kind of relationship find that their special issues and problems are, in fact, *common* issues and problems.

Contrary to a prevailing misconception, membership in a Covenant Discipleship group, for example, is not the prerogative of the spiritual elite. Quite the contrary. Support groups are for those of us who *need support—*

and in the life of the Spirit, that means most of us. The practice of spiritual direction, one-on-one, has for centuries been an effective form of support and accountability, particularly in the Roman Catholic tradition; but for most people, private spiritual direction is, if desirable, not very feasible. Therefore the promise of the Holy Spirit to provide guidance and inspiration wherever the faithful few are gathered in Christ's name is one the church must take seriously. The class meeting structure has been referred to before as a form of group spiritual guidance and, indeed, can be precisely that.

What distinguishes the class meeting model from many other forms of spiritual support groups is the strong emphasis on personal accountability. The one hour spent together each week is a time not simply for sharing something mutually edifying, but for rendering an account to the covenant community of the current state of our relationship with God. Now why, you might ask, would anyone want to do that? Isn't my relationship with God purely private? The church says no.

Privacy is a prime cultural value in American society, and the strict, constitutionally supported separation of church and state in this country has created a cultural climate in which religion is habitually seen as an entirely individual matter—an issue of personal choice. This relegation of religion to the private sphere has resulted in the increasing secularization of American culture and contributed to suppressing the public nature of Christian witness—so evident in both scripture and tradition—in the lives of most communities and congregations. Thus, lifelong Christians not only feel shy about sharing their faith with the unchurched; many of them feel equally inhibited about sharing their religious beliefs, their doubts, and their struggles to follow Christ faithfully, even (or especially!) within their own local churches. As a result, many Christians who surround themselves with friends and busy themselves frantically with church activities are nevertheless on very lonely spiritual pilgrimages. They are going on to perfection alone.

Part of the problem derives from a common tendency to confuse intimacy and privacy. It is true that our relationship with God is—or should be—an extremely intimate exchange. But the degree of intimacy we seek with God is no barrier to sharing our faith and spiritual practice with a fellow traveler. Quite the contrary: As we become increasingly secure in this relationship, we can be increasingly "public" about it. The point is not that we are all meant to become aggressive evangelists, pressing our own religious enthusiasms on the religiously indifferent or hostile. It is much more a matter of being always prepared to "have your answer ready for people who ask you the reason for the hope that you all have"—for the hungry ones Grace will inevitably put in your path (I Pet. 3:15). And ask you they will. Once you have submitted yourself to the pressure of the Potter's hand, your quest will no longer be a solitary one. The fitly turned vessel, filled to the brim with the love of God, must and will find a way of sharing that love.

The actual logistics of beginning and maintaining a class meeting or Covenant Discipleship group in the local church setting are fairly simple and have been laid out in detail by David Lowes Watson, Executive Secretary of Covenant Discipleship and Christian Formation, in *Accountable Discipleship: Handbook for Covenant Discipleship Groups in the Congregation,* a publication of the General Board of Discipleship of The United Methodist Church. (For other helpful resources, see the list that follows this postscript.) But the fact that the structure and procedures for implementing this model are simple should not be allowed to obscure the reality that the kind of long-term commitment to God and to one another that the task requires can be very difficult indeed. Once the initial glow has faded and the novelty has worn off, the promise to be "publically" faithful to a mutually agreed upon set of spiritual practices can begin to seem burdensome, particularly if their primary function as a means of grace is lost sight of. The temptation quickly to turn the group into one that simply shares and supports without calling to account can become almost irresistible. Or, in some cases, the opposite problem may arise: The issue of accountability becomes so predominant that a form of legalism emerges. In this instance, the covenant which holds the group together ceases to function as a spiritual bond and, instead, degenerates into a series of rules and regulations. Those who are successful in following them take comfort in being "good" Christians. Those who are not successful fall away. Both problems are a consequence of the failure to understand the spiritual life as a relationship.

In the deepest part of each one of us, whether we acknowledge it or not, is a longing for God nothing else can satisfy. It was there the moment we drew our first breath and will be there when we breathe our last. Let us take heart, then, in the Good News that as deep and insatiable as our longing may be, God's longing *for us* is deeper yet and still more insatiable. The hard truth is that the very first steps we take on the straight and narrow path to perfection will almost certainly be halting and painful. But equally true is that Christian perfection is a well-traveled path. Many souls have gone before and left us countless maps and guides as forms of encouragement. If we, like Paul, can keep our eyes on the prize to be won rather than on the distance that separates us from it, we will be amazed at what we see: God running, with outstretched arms, ready to embrace us.

Resources for Laity

For those interested in pursuing the possibility of mutual accountability in the spiritual life, the following resources are recommended:

Essential:

The Covenant Discipleship Quarterly. Published by the Office of Covenant Discipleship and Christian Formation at the General Board of Discipleship of The United Methodist Church, P. O. Box 840, Nashville, TN 37202-0840. Annual Subscription: eight dollars.

Watson, David Lowes. *Accountable Discipleship: Handbook for Covenant Discipleship Groups in the Congregation.* Nashville: Discipleship Resources, 1984.

———. *The Early Methodist Class Meeting.* Nashville: Discipleship Resources, 1985.

Highly Recommended:

Chilcote, Paul Wesley. *Wesley Speaks on Christian Vocation.* Nashville: Discipleship Resources, 1986.

Harper, Steve. *Devotional Life in the Wesleyan Tradition.* Nashville: The Upper Room, 1983.

Martin, John R. *Ventures in Discipleship: A Handbook for Groups or Individuals*. Scottdale, Pa.: Herald Press, 1984.

Olsen, Charles M. *Cultivating Religious Growth Groups*. Philadelphia: Westminster Press, 1984.

Christian Perfection in Preaching, Teaching, and Counseling

Some Issues for Pastors, Seminarians, and Theological Educators to Reflect On

The ideal of Christian perfection and the spiritual practices associated with it are frequently new—even alien—to many entering seminarians. They often report that their experience in the local church has not only not reinforced this central focus of Wesleyan spirituality but has for the most part bypassed basic soteriological doctrines altogether. Terms such as "justification," "sanctification," "holiness," or "atonement" sound foreign or archaic. Even the word *salvation* has become suspect, perhaps because it has been used so freely—and, hence, made trivial—by popular religious leaders in the media.

When I raise the issue with my students, the response I usually get goes something like this: Traditional theological—especially soteriological—language is not used in the local church because it is no longer "relevant." Since the words are essentially meaningless to today's Christian, it is pointless to try to use them. No one would understand what you are talking about. The (usually unspoken) assumption is that the contemporary situation demands a new vocabulary in which to communicate the gospel. Perhaps. But this argument overlooks that the average layperson is usually very familiar with technical terms in areas of compelling personal interest: medicine, sports, science, economics, or psychotherapy—to name a few. The general populace can and does appropriate technical language when it sees that it is in its interest to do so. Given this reality, it is difficult to avoid the conclusion that traditional language is no longer "relevant" or comprehensible, because the issue of salvation is itself no longer seen as personally compelling—at least by those who govern the choice of theological language in denominations, seminaries, and local congregations.

If the "relevance" argument is valid, then it presupposes the possibility of establishing a more adequate set of soteriological terms: either that or a new doctrine of salvation. And therein lies the rub. According to some sociolinguists, in order to experience a reality we must have a word for it. This school of thought, reflected in the recent work of theologian George Lindbeck, maintains that although there are "non-reflective experiences, there are no uninterpreted or unschematized ones." Lindbeck, whose book *The Nature of Doctrine* (Westminster Press, 1984) has caused an enormous stir in academic circles, has based his theory of the priority of religious language (tradition) over religious experience on just such an argument:

> On this view, the means of communication and expression are a precondition, a kind of quasi-transcendental (i.e., culturally formed) *a priori* for the possibility of experience. We cannot identify, describe, or recognize experience qua experience without the use of signs and symbols. These are necessary even for what the depth psychologist speaks of as "unconscious" or "subconscious" experiences, or for what the phenomenologist describes as prereflective ones. In short,

> it is necessary to have the means for expressing an
> experience in order to have it, and the richer our
> expressive or linguistic system, the more subtle varied,
> and differentiated can be our experience. (pp. 36-37)

For a religious tradition that makes such strong claims
for the necessity and authority of religious experience,
the argument—right or wrong—is a crucial one. If
Lindbeck and the sociolinguists are correct, the
language of salvation needs to be rich, varied, and
complex if the experience of salvation is to be likewise. If
we do not have a word for it, we are not going to
experience the precise reality. Therefore, the proposi-
tion that we can or should substitute new terms for old
must be looked at carefully.

What will be the long-term effect of eliminating words
such as *perfection, holiness,* or *sanctification* from the
operating vocabulary of contemporary Christians? By
abandoning traditional soteriological terms will we, in
effect, be cutting ourselves off from a particular kind of
religious experience? Have we succeeded in finding
adequate substitutes for the traditional terms? If so,
what are they? Or does the abandonment of traditional
soteriological language actually signal the abandonment
of the soteriological doctrines the terms identify? Has
the understandable liberal distaste for simplistic religious formulations resulted in losing the game by a kind
of theological default? (If *that's* what they mean by
"holiness," then let there be no more talk of "holiness"!)
What will be the consequences for a distinctive
Wesleyan denominational identity if the traditional
language of salvation is rejected?

This particular concern has surfaced for me—and no

doubt for others in my profession—as a consequence of
my reading personal theological statements written by
students preparing to leave seminary and enter
ordained ministry. More often than not, those portions
of their papers that deal with the subject of salvation are
notably vague and imprecise. Feeling uncomfortable
with words such as *sin* and *holiness,* seminarians have
substituted terms such as "brokenness" and "aliena-
tion," or "wholeness" and *"shalom."* That the word *sin*
should give rise to discomfort is not surprising. Its
connotations seem harsh, judgmental, and uncompro-
mising. But to substitute terms that accurately describe
the *consequences* of sin for sin itself, has the effect of
dissolving the element of personal accountability.
Similarly, discomfort with the word *holiness* can be
attributed to particular historical developments that led
ultimately to sectarian divisions among Methodists. For
many, "holiness" has come to mean a set of concrete and
restrictive social mores that have little to do with one's
stance before God. But while "holiness" implies
"wholeness," wholeness does not convey emphatically
the sense of ultimacy, mystery, and (yes) *terror* that
hovers around the word *holy.* Nor does *shalom,* a
theologically important and attractive word in biblical
studies, suggest the extent to which radical risk is
entailed in the issues of salvation. The point is not that
words such as *brokenness* or *shalom* should not be used;
they should. But they should not be employed as
palatable euphemisms replacing the more explicit
traditional language. A starkly truncated theological
vocabulary results in an equally truncated doctrine of

salvation, and where so much is at stake the church cannot afford to veil the reality.

Alongside the issue of traditional theological language goes the question of resources. We are accustomed to claiming that scripture and other traditional and authoritative theological sources are "culturally conditioned," and so they are. The claim is further made that their cultural specificity limits their effectiveness. This, too, is often true. What we are much less likely to recognize, however, is the extent to which *we* are culturally conditioned. Do we and the people we serve have to have everything presented in contemporary language or contexts in order to be able to hear and appreciate it? What are the likely consequences of our abandoning the pre–twentieth-century spiritual resources of our faith? Might such a rash decision, in effect, serve to make us even more parochial than we may already be? Are we secure enough to be able to meet the older texts and receive what they have to offer without taking constant personal offense and having to engage in a kind of psychological warfare with them? John Wesley's attitude was to take whatever he could fruitfully use. We also need to learn to take what we can use, and simply let *be* that which we cannot come to terms with. We may find in future years that what once seemed useless and incomprehensible has finally become indispensable.

The doctrine of Christian perfection is challenging and demanding. We must ask ourselves, where in our preaching, teaching, and counseling are we willing to challenge people? Are we willing to confront Christians on issues relating to peace and justice? to personal morality? to forms of self-indulgence? to disciplined forms of prayer and devotion? What are the areas we find ourselves consciously or unconsciously avoiding? Specifically, how do we deal with the issue of sin?

As a soteriological doctrine, Christian perfection assumes the central significance of the individual's personal relationship with God. How much practical assistance are we willing or able to offer people who want to learn how to pray with greater fervor and faithfulness? Have we found a way of talking about or modeling being in personal relationship to Jesus Christ that does justice to the elements of love, obedience, and moral accountability? If we feel weak in these areas, what efforts have we made to gain the needed experience and expertise?

What structures can be developed in the congregation to support the understanding of salvation that the doctrine of Christian perfection suggests? If most congregations have not yet been introduced to the Covenant Discipleship model (an effort to reclaim the structure of the early Methodist class meeting sponsored by The United Methodist Board of Discipleship), how might we begin to prepare the ground for this in preaching? What kind of reception would this model of spiritual practice likely receive without such preparation? What sort of liturgical support for this model might be developed?

The question of implementing a spiritual vision in the concrete structures of congregational life is complex and socially sensitive. The formative culture in which the American church now finds itself is pervasively individualistic and hedonistic, and a general call to live a

Christian life is unlikely to effect radical change. As in preceding epochs, the church will need to spell out with much greater specificity than it has been willing to do recently just what a Christian life-style entails—what "going on to perfection" in the late twentieth century really means. The problem will not be solved simply by teaching a Lenten study on Christian perfection, though this might be a helpful place to begin. What we have to recognize is that the issues of salvation must be dealt with over and over again in a wide variety of settings before they can become pervasive and personally compelling. The church has done this before. With God's help the church can do it again; and the spiritual practice of John Wesley suggests that it may yet be possible to stress individual accountability (as in the practice of spiritual disciplines) within the broader community we call "the communion of saints."

— CHRISTIAN PERFECTION IN — CHRISTIAN TRADITION

Sources for a Wesleyan Spirituality

The following authors were important influences on the development of John Wesley's doctrine of Christian perfection and his spiritual practice:

I. *Particularly Influential Sources*

Gregory of Nyssa (via Macarius the Egyptian)
Ephraim Syrus
Thomas a Kempis, *The Imitation of Christ*
Jeremy Taylor, *The Rule and Exercises of Holy Living and Holy Dying.*
William Law, *A Serious Call to a Devout and Holy Life* (See also *The Spirit of Love*)

II. *Patristic Sources*

Clement of Rome
Ignatius of Antioch
Polycarp
Justin Martyr
Irenaeus
Origen

Clement of Alexandria
Cyprian
Augustine
Basil of Cappadocia
John Chrysostom

III. *Roman Catholic Mystics*

Brother Lawrence of the Resurrection
Pascal
François Fénelon
Quesnel
Scupoli
de Renty
Mme. Guyon
Mme. Bourignon
John of the Cross
Lopez
Molinos
Tauler
Theologica Germanica

BIBLIOGRAPHY

Flew, R. Newton. *The Idea of Perfection in Christian Theology*. London: Humphrey Milford and Oxford University Press, 1934.

Garrigou-Lagrange, Réginald, O.P. *Christian Perfection and Contemplation According to St. Thomas Aquinas and St. John of the Cross*. Trans. Sr. Timothea Doyle, O.P. St. Louis, Mo., and London: B. Herder Book Co., 1937.

————. *The Three Ages of the Interior Life: Prelude of Eternal Life*. Trans. Sr. Timothea Doyle, O.P. St. Louis, Mo., and London: B. Herder Book Co., 1949.

Lindstrom, Harald. *Wesley and Sanctification*. Wilmore, Ky.: Francis Asbury Publishing Co., n.d.

Passmore, John. *The Perfectibility of Man*. New York: Charles Scribner's Sons, 1970.

Sangster, W. E. *The Path to Perfection: An Examination and Restatement of John Wesley's Doctrine of Christian Perfection*. London: Epworth Press, 1943.

————. *The Pure in Heart: A Study in Christian Sanctity*. Nashville: Abingdon Press, 1943, reissued in 1984.

Stolz, Anselm, O.S.B. *The Doctrine of Spiritual Perfection*. Trans. Aidan Williams, O.S.B. St. Louis, Mo., and London: B. Herder Book Co., 1938.